LEADERSHIP
MATTERS

PETER BAINES

LEADERSHIP MATTERS

STORIES AND INSIGHTS FOR **LEADERS, ACHIEVERS,** AND **VISIONARIES**

WILEY

First published in 2023 by John Wiley & Sons Australia, Ltd
Level 4, 600 Bourke St, Melbourne Victoria 3000, Australia

Typeset in Plantin Std Regular 11.5/16.5pt

© Soulful Experiences Pty Ltd 2023

The moral rights of the author have been asserted

ISBN: 978-1-394-17697-7

A catalogue record for this book is available from the National Library of Australia

Cover design by Wiley

Cover Image: © elenabs / Getty Images

Disclaimer

The material in this publication is of the nature of general comment only, and does not represent professional advice. It is not intended to provide specific guidance for particular circumstances and it should not be relied on as the basis for any decision to take action or not take action on any matter which it covers. Readers should obtain professional advice where appropriate, before making any such decision. To the maximum extent permitted by law, the author and publisher disclaim all responsibility and liability to any person, arising directly or indirectly from any person taking or not taking action based on the information in this publication.

To CT, the journey without you would be slow, boring and likely predictable.

CONTENTS

About the author   ix

Acknowledgements   xiii

Introduction   xv

Part I: The Leaders   1

1   Focus on results, not excuses   3

2   Meet unique challenges with unique solutions   21

3   Embrace courageous leadership   37

4   Be present and show you care   51

5   Leave a lasting impression   67

Part II: The Achievers   81

6   Manage risk, don't fear it   83

7   Model a life well lived   103

8   Believe in the future   117

9   Find clarity through action   129

Part III: The Visionaries   149

10 Find a journey that feeds your soul   151

11 Engage heart, head and hands   169

12 Plan your exit strategy from day one   189

13 Adopt a limitless mindset   203

Conclusion   *217*

Thai names and places   *221*

About Hands   *225*

ABOUT THE AUTHOR

Peter Baines OAM, one of Australia's foremost leadership experts, has road-tested leadership the hard way. In his 22 years with the NSW Police he led teams responding to acts of terrorism and natural disasters on a scale not previously experienced by Australian police.

Peter was part of the leadership team that travelled to Bali in the aftermath of the bombings in 2002, and in early 2005 he was called to lead international teams in response to the Boxing Day tsunami in South-East Asia. He headed up multiple rotations into Thailand tasked with identifying those who had died. His leadership theories were fully tested in this harrowing environment.

After witnessing the devastating effects of the tsunami, creating sustainable leadership became a passion. Having been especially deeply touched by the number of children left without parents by the disaster, he was inspired to set up an organisation that could make a real difference in the lives of these children. In late 2005 he founded *Hands Across the Water* to raise funds for, and awareness about, the orphaned children of Thailand.

Hands has raised more than $30 million to date. They have built several children's homes across Thailand, purchased a rubber plantation to create a sustainable and regular income, constructed a community centre in the Khao Lak region of Thailand and a Digital Learning Centre in the northeast. The charity now has operations in seven different locations in Thailand and provides a home for several hundred children every night, but its main focus is on the long-term future of the children and the communities in which they live. They have also supported more than 30 children through university, all of whom have graduated and look forward to a life of choice rather than chance.

A unique approach of the charity has been their focus on creating meaningful shared experiences for their supporters, and a cornerstone event on their calendar is the long-distance bike rides in Thailand that Peter leads throughout the year.

His final years with the NSW Police were spent on secondment to the National Institute of Forensic Science, where he worked on national and international capacity-building projects around counterterrorism and leadership. He spent time advising Interpol in France and the United Nations Office on Drugs and Crime in South-East Asia.

Peter was engaged by the Government of Saudi Arabia following the deadly floods in Jeddah in 2010 to review their response and provide advice on crisis mitigation and leadership. In 2011 he deployed to Japan in response to the tsunami that claimed thousands of lives there.

Peter has received numerous awards, including an Order of Australia Medal in 2014, for his international humanitarian work. In 2016 he was awarded the Most Admirable Order of the Direkgunabhorn (Fifth Class) by the King of Thailand. In 2010 he was a NSW finalist at the Australian of the Year awards. He was the first Australian to be awarded the international honour of a Rotary Professional Excellence Award in 2008. He received the NSW Police Service Medal and the Australian Federal Police Operations Medal for his work in Asia.

He was the first NSW Police Officer to be awarded the Humanitarian Overseas Service Medal and Australian National Medal. He has completed university studies in Law and Forensic Science and postgraduate studies in Management.

Today Peter helps businesses build effective sustainable leadership programs through the unique mix of his leadership and corporate social responsibility initiatives. He is Director of International Operations for *Hands Across the Water* and sits on a number of boards.

Peter has written two previous books, *Hands Across the Water*, published by Pan MacMillan, and *Doing Good by Doing Good*, published by Wiley.

Peter has three adult children, Lachie, Kels and Jack, and one grandchild, little Patrick. Peter and his wife Claire divide their time between their farm in the Capertee Valley and Terrigal on the Central Coast. In addition to their continued focus on supporting the kids and communities of Thailand through *Hands*, Peter and Claire have established an ecotourism business, welcoming guests to what they call the meeting point between the stunning natural environment and modern luxury.

In all that Peter and Claire do they are ably assisted by their springer spaniels Burton and Frankie.

You can connect with peter via email peter@peterbaines.com.au

ACKNOWLEDGEMENTS

These acknowledgements are less about the writing of the book and more about those who have contributed to the experiences that have given me the opportunity to write again.

If our best experiences in life are those shared then I am blessed to share life and all that it offers with my wife, Claire. Each adventure we take on is more achievable and enjoyable when we face it together. You bring compassion, empathy and a beautiful soul to all that we do. My worth and personal share price rose when you joined me and everyone is grateful for that.

Lachie, Rea and Little Patty, Kels and Josh, Jack and Jords, life is just quite simply better with all of you guys and I can't imagine it without you. Chris and Wendy, thank you. Life and all that we face is achievable with your support, without it, I'm not so sure.

There are few people who have contributed more to my life since the formation of *Hands* than Kay Spencer, our chairman. Your devotion to the children and communities of Thailand is second to none and a more loyal person would be hard to find. You see beyond the faults and transgressions that we make in life, and always look for and believe in the best in people.

The past and present decision makers of the members and suppliers of the Narta group who, since 2007 and the San Francisco conference, have supported *Hands* beyond measure. The balance is unevenly tipped in our favour in the flow of value, but the positive change you have brought to the lives of so many is immeasurable.

The past and present board members of *Hands* in Australia, New Zealand and Thailand, thank you for the contribution to improving the lives of those we choose to support.

Dale and Katherine Beaumont. In 2013 you made a very personal and professional decision to support *Hands* and bring your immense talents to our cause. You connect business with social impact and in doing so create positive futures for your community and that of *Hands*.

To the many members of the real estate industry who choose to travel to Thailand and ride with us, you bring positive change to the lives of the kids and communities.

Each and every contributor to *Hands* is valued. Since our first ride in 2009 we have been fortunate to welcome hundreds of riders and thousands of supporters into the *Hands* community. Without the riders and without their supporters we're unable to do what we do. It's a humbling experience to watch the community grow based on our contributions.

I offer my deep appreciation to those who have made a positive contribution to the work of *Hands*. My commitment is to continue to explore ways to bring positive change to the lives of the children and communities we support.

Finally, I very much appreciate the support of the entire team at Wiley who got this from a concept to a book. Thank you.

INTRODUCTION

I don't believe that we can have life experiences without the opportunity to learn from them, though much will depend on whether or not we are open to the learning. My experience is that the best learnings happen outside the classroom. It is often when life gets messy, complicated, even a bit dirty, that we learn the most about ourselves and about those around us.

In *Leadership Matters*, I share with you a collection of my own learnings from the rich experiences I have been fortunate to enjoy. It is the people I have shared those experiences with who have contributed most to my learnings. Many of these lessons were not obvious to me at the time; it is only when I have taken time to reflect that I have recognised the blessed life I have been offered.

The book is broken into three parts to focus on, respectively, Leaders, Achievers and Visionaries. Part I looks at how a range of courageous Leaders, faced with difficult circumstances, have navigated those challenges. I examine the contexts and the unique solutions they applied.

When their progress runs up against overwhelming odds, sometimes against logic, the Achievers get the job done. In Part II we'll review how they succeed, not because of the absence of challenge or fear, but because they are determined to overcome it. They keep going when others would quit. They're not afraid to take risks or make mistakes, because they understand that doing so is part of the learning process and of every success story.

In Part III we meet the Visionaries. They are the vanguard leaders who will meet the challenges of our times. They view life and leadership with fresh eyes, unconstrained by received wisdom and convention, actively challenging their own and others' preconceived limitations. They understand the importance of self, of feeding our soul, and the value of meaningful shared experiences.

In *Leadership Matters*, my third book, I document the lessons I have learned that I consider most important in building strong leaders. Importantly, I challenge the increasing prevalence in organisations of risk avoidance. We can always find reasons not to do something, but I have learned that some of our greatest achievements depend on our waiving the rules and stepping outside the boundaries imposed by others.

I worked with the NSW Police for 22 years, the major portion of that time devoted to the Forensic Services Command investigating major crime scenes, suspicious deaths and matters likely to appear before the coroner or supreme courts. Internationally, I contributed to the forensic investigations of both the Bali bombings in 2002 and the Boxing Day tsunami in 2004.

My work in Thailand in the aftermath of the tsunami would have the biggest impact on my personal and professional life and shape their future direction. I had worked outside of Australia in the area of counterterrorism before leaving the police to focus on the charity *Hands Across the Water*, which I founded in 2005 to support children in Thailand left without parents.

Leaving the police to establish *Hands* would introduce me to a life in which I discovered that the richest rewards flowed from giving without expectation. I was soon invited to share my personal experiences and stories of leadership on stages across the globe, which in turn helped to support the change we could achieve in Thailand.

This book is directed at current or aspiring leaders, but not solely so. The contextual leadership lessons can be readily incorporated into your own personal life, whether or not you see yourself as a leader. One of the most valuable take-aways in this book is the invitation to *just start*.

I have witnessed death and tragedy in my professional career on a scale that separates me from the overwhelming majority of the population. If there has been one gift from that exposure to the worst of humanity it has been to witness the best of humanity. I have also learned that *we need to enjoy what we do or change what we do*. To live a life with our greatest dreams unrealised is to settle for a lesser life than we owe ourselves and those we love.

PART I

THE LEADERS

Leaders choose to write their own story rather than leaving it to others. They challenge the rules that others accept without question. They are creative, innovative, and step forward when others step back.

These leaders make themselves known when we're presented with unique challenges. They embrace the difficult and the darkness to bring clarity and light. They see crisis and disaster as testing grounds for true leadership.

You will remember them. They leave lasting impressions not necessarily because of their advanced technical skills but because they care about people. Their goal is to build for the greater good rather than for personal reward. They look to take others on the journey with them, rather than forging ahead alone in search of glory.

CHAPTER I
FOCUS ON RESULTS, NOT EXCUSES

There will always be a reason to decide not to do something, and there will always be people who offer up excuses. My advice? Focus on results and let others focus on the excuses. When we embark on a journey that truly feeds our soul, whatever that might be, it's funny how often we find a way to succeed despite the thousands of reasons, logical and less so, why we shouldn't.

When Gill, a colleague from the Thames Valley Police in the UK with whom I worked during my third rotation into Thailand, asked me if I wanted to help support a group of kids in Thailand who were without family or home, saying 'yes' didn't seem that big a deal to me. To be honest, it probably didn't make much sense given the personal circumstances I found myself in at the time, and even on reflection it doesn't make a lot of sense, but I'm glad I did it.

During my tours to Thailand in 2005 my marriage had come to an end and I found myself living a financially challenged life. We had three kids in private school and a decent mortgage without a lot of excess once the bills were paid. So adding the rent and running costs of a second home without a change in income was at best an exercise in creative accounting. After the bills were paid I was left with $80 a fortnight to live on, which included feeding the kids when I had them. I was still working in the police full time, and due to my rank as a Police Inspector I no longer had the opportunity to earn overtime, so what I had was *all* I had.

The truth is, at the time of starting *Hands* my personal life could not have been in a more dire state. I was at the lowest point in my life — mentally, physically and financially broken. But for some reason making a commitment to help the kids of Thailand left without parents seemed the right thing to do. As it turned out, the positive effect *Hands* has had on my life is immeasurable and I will be eternally grateful for the gift it has given me.

So, for whatever reason, when Gill posed the question, saying yes just seemed like the right answer. Over the years I've had many conversations with people who have assumed that setting up the organisation was a way of dealing with the trauma of working in Thailand, that in some way it was a therapeutic exercise for me. That might sound logical, but quite simply it wasn't the truth.

I had spent my entire professional life dealing with victims and their families who have suffered the kind of loss that most families thankfully will never have to encounter. And the further my career progressed, the greater the scale of loss I was dealing with.

Very early on in my police career, my partner and I had less than five years' experience between us. We were both just 22 years old, so very junior in the force and, dare I say it, in lived life experience. Not long after starting night shift at Cabramatta Police Station we were called to the scene of motor vehicle collision at the intersection of the Hume Highway and Cabramatta Road.

It was a 'persons trapped' accident, a direct result of high speed and an inexperienced driver. Both occupants of the vehicle were trapped but released in a critical condition and taken to nearby Liverpool Hospital.

The driver died as a result of his injuries on the way to hospital, which meant that among our other duties we had to deliver the death message to his parents. Since they were living apart this meant delivering the message twice. We also took family members to the mortuary for the formal identification process, and as we returned to the patrol car the police radio advised that the second occupant of the vehicle had also died.

We would deliver two further death messages before our shift was over, the last to one of the parents who was a school teacher and that message had to be delivered at his place of work. I recall that as I was expressing my deep regret for his loss, with words spoken for the fourth time in one shift my partner had tears running down her face. My voice was breaking and I was doing all I could to remain composed.

Driving back to the station after delivering the last of the four messages, I felt empty. It was late in the morning, some 12 hours since our shift had started. I was physically and emotionally spent. Many years later I would learn in Thailand from people who had endured the worst losses imaginable that the most difficult days I would face would be dealing with families; and the most rewarding days would be dealing with families.

Joining the NSW Police as a 19-year-old I could never have imagined the opportunities that would come my way. I spent the first four and a half years working in uniform, with the first 12 months at Merrylands Police Station before I requested a transfer to neighbouring Cabramatta. I left Merrylands because it offered what many seek in life: a quiet area with a low crime rate where you could see out your eight-hour shift without too many incidents. An attractive place to work, then, unless you're a 19-year-old straight out of the academy looking for anything but safe and quiet. Cabramatta offered everything that Merrylands didn't. It certainly wasn't quiet, and not altogether safe. It wasn't safe for the rival drug gangs, or necessarily safe for those of us in a blue uniform. I sustained a broken arm and a broken nose that saw me hospitalised and requiring surgery after a car chase and a wrestle with some crooks, but I loved my time at Cabramatta—until I didn't.

The most difficult days I would face would be dealing with families; and the most rewarding days would be dealing with families.

The move into the forensic area in the Crime Scene Unit appealed on many levels. It got me out of uniform and out of the western suburbs where I was no longer living, and it offered an opportunity to specialise in an area that I had found of huge interest. I spent the first 18 months working at the Sydney Police Centre focusing on major crime scenes within the Sydney CBD before an opportunity arose to head bush. I spent the next 10 years living and working in Tamworth in the Crime Scene Section before returning to where my time in the forensic area had started, back at the Sydney Police Centre. When I walked through the doors at the beginning of 2002, however, I was a Detective Inspector in charge of a number of crime scene units and other specialist areas, including the one I was returning to.

I had been promoted to the rank of Inspector at the age of 35, which was not the norm. Several circumstances had worked in my favour. The specialist nature of the job I was doing meant the field of suitable and qualified applicants was very small, keeping competition to a minimum, and a restructure had seen a number of positions created at the same time.

Things couldn't have presented better for me, but that didn't mean I felt I had all the answers. With a healthy dose of imposter syndrome I returned to the office I had started out at and each day turned up with the belief that if I could help others do their job I was doing my job. I thrived in the role—the challenges, the freedom, the opportunity to bring about change, and working with keen younger people was refreshing.

Waking up to the news of the Bali bombings I felt an immediate desire to be part of the response. It was certainly the biggest event that had occurred in my career, and after all I had specialised in this area for over a decade. I was duly offered the opportunity to deploy to Bali as part of the multi-jurisdictional leadership team tasked with identification of the victims, including Australian, Indonesian and other foreign nationals. My time in Bali exposed me to the identification process and allowed me to work as part of an international deployment. More than that, it positioned me for deployment to Thailand in the aftermath of the Boxing Day tsunami two years later.

Boxing Day. The day after. For many it is the day that follows what is a day of celebration and overindulgence, likely a ridiculously early start if you have kids in the house under 10, and time with family. It's also day one of the Melbourne Test and good reason for all cricket lovers to find a comfy lounge chair and settle in.

As the first session in the cricket came to an end, what has been identified as the third biggest earthquake ever recorded struck off the northern tip of Sumatra in Indonesia. The movement of the tectonic plates triggered a tsunami that would travel across the Indian Ocean at a speed of 800 kilometres an hour before it reached the coastlines of Indonesia, Sri Lanka, Thailand and other countries. An estimated 250 000 lives would be lost as a direct result.

I had never been to Thailand, but as I watched the breaking news of the tsunami and the growing death toll I knew I wanted to go. The desire to step into a scene of mass death and destruction might not seem a rational one, or likely to be shared by many. But when you have trained for it your entire career, it is natural to want to be part of the solution.

It was a deep honour to be invited to join the Australian team that travelled to Thailand to assist in the reuniting of families. Across multiple rotations I would form a deep attachment to the country and people of Thailand, one that I could previously never have imagined. Starting *Hands Across the Water* in 2005 to assist a group of children who had lost their families was not a well-planned decision, nor was it an exercise in personal therapy, as some would later speculate. It simply seemed like the right thing for me to do at the time. With my personal life in the toilet, I was struggling on all fronts to do the little things right, and trying to find my way to be a dad to my kids, but I was failing continually and spectacularly on multiple fronts.

The desire to step into a scene of mass death and destruction might not seem a logical one, or likely to be shared by many. But when you have trained for it your entire career, it is natural to want to be part of the solution.

During my last tour of Thailand I had been asked by the Royal Thai Police to lead a three-month recovery project on Phi Phi

Island that would see the excavation of a collapsed sea wall where it was believed unrecovered bodies might be found. The idea of hiding away from all of my problems on Phi Phi Island for three months appealed, but I knew that the decision makers within NSW Police would simply laugh at the idea of allowing me to return to Thailand, having now spent several months there through the course of 2005.

Returning to the Forensic Services Command in late 2005, after almost a year consumed by the tsunami efforts either on or offshore, I felt lost, without direction and purpose. The position I had occupied prior to Thailand had been filled and I was turning up to work each day effectively without a job to do. I had gone from leading the Australian and International teams during my deployments to Thailand to riding sidecar with the office admin clerk. I had lost the office I occupied, and with it any meaningful sense of purpose. My reintegration into 'normal' life after my international work hadn't gone well on any level.

The irony was not lost on me that at a time when I was pretty much at rock bottom on all levels of my life I was starting to present on the corporate speaking circuit, sharing lessons on life, leadership and purpose. I did what I have always done: I turned up with a huge case of imposter syndrome and carried on regardless. Imagining that each speaking event I did would be the last. But they kept coming, and I had found a platform to talk about *Hands* and the work I was doing in Thailand.

I did what I have always done: I turned up with a huge case of imposter syndrome and carried on regardless.

A psychologist I would see many years later when attempting to unwind more mess and hurt I had created told me I had 'a big ego and low self-esteem'. I rationalised that the speaking I was doing and the standing ovations I received were stroking my ego, but there was this constant lack of confidence and belief that I wasn't good enough and looked for validation.

The speaking was serving many needs I had then. It was feeding my ego and giving me the validation I was seeking, but more importantly, it gave *Hands* a platform and was a significant source of donations and connections. The year 2006 saw me rise rapidly from the depths into which I had sunk both personally and professionally, and much of that was made possible by my saying 'yes' to starting *Hands* when on every logical level the timing didn't make sense.

That year I was invited to apply for a secondment to the National Institute of Forensic Science (NIFS) to lead a research project for Interpol in France linked to terrorism with a focus on chemical, biological, radiological and nuclear (CBRN) threats and trends. Working out of NSW Police, I was to split my time between the Melbourne office of NIFS and Interpol in Lyon, France. It was purely a research role with no operational activities, and with hindsight the timing couldn't have been better. I worked closely with Dr Tony Raymond, one of the most dedicated scientists I have ever met, and this role gave me freedom and a sense of purpose.

The role with NIFS also allowed me to take up the increasing number of speaking opportunities that were arising. Tony didn't mind when I did my research work and had no attachment to an eight-hour workday. He could see the progress of the research, the hours I was investing and the balancing of growing demands, and he supported me on all levels. Where needed I was taking annual leave to pursue speaking jobs and worked late into each night on the growth of *Hands*. I was handwriting receipts to all donors and physically posting them out. Clearly that couldn't be sustained.

The agreement with NSW Police was for a 12-month secondment, but towards the end of the year Tony lobbied for an additional year, as I had by then been invited to spend time working with and advising the UN Office on Drugs and Crime in South-East Asia. The additional secondment was approved and I continued to grow further and further away from the role I had left in NSW Police. From the time I left Australia for Thailand in January of 2005, I never returned to the job I had occupied. For the next four years I spent more time working with international agencies than at home.

I have seen one consistently recurring phenomenon: lots of people from the government and corporate sectors, NGOs and charities sweep in to help in the aftermath of the crisis, but too many of them leave too soon.

During my years with NIFS, working with Interpol and the UN, *Hands* continued to grow, as did my speaking opportunities, which hit an all-time high in 2008 when I delivered more than 100 keynotes while still working full-time. All this left little meaningful time for other obligations, sadly including my kids. But the more I spoke at conferences, the more money I was raising for the kids in Thailand, which allowed us to provide assistance on a larger scale. We opened more community centres, which meant we needed more recurrent funding and I needed to spend more time working on *Hands*.

In the international work I have done in the aftermath of crises and disasters in Indonesia, Thailand, Saudi Arabia and Japan, I have seen one consistently recurring phenomenon: lots of people from the government and corporate sectors, NGOs and charities swoop in to help in the aftermath of the crisis, but too many of them leave too soon.

On the ground in Thailand in 2005, when I was still walking around the villages and communities in my police uniform, long before starting *Hands*, I visited buildings erected by global charities without consultation with the local community. Now those who had built them had moved on, these buildings were neither needed nor wanted.

Hands Across the Water was late to the party, we didn't open our first home until 2006. It was built for the 32 kids I had met in the tent at the local temple the previous year. Within 12 months of opening that first home the numbers had doubled. We had girls sleeping three to a bed; the boys were sleeping on the floor and the question we asked ourselves was *where were they coming from?* It was now a couple of years on from the tsunami, but each time I arrived there seemed to be more kids without families or options. We opened our second home in January 2009, but each new building brought more kids and increased costs.

I started *Hands* with the intention of building and sustaining a home for those kids I had met at the temple. Naively I believed that if we built them a home their problems would be solved. Ten years after the tsunami *Hands* had grown to support seven different communities and homes across Thailand. Our original home at Baan Tharn Namchai had grown from a single home in 2006 to what is now a village. There was now a building for the boys, one for the girls and one built specifically for the babies and younger children, as required by the Thai Government. The growth in the number of kids at Baan Tharn Namchai could be put down to a number of factors.

In the years that followed the tsunami a number of homes like ours were opened to meet a need not unlike the one we were serving. There were both private initiatives through the not-for-profit (NFP) sector and government-funded buildings. As time passed, interest in the needs of the community receded—and so too did the funding. Over the years I visited a number of private homes, similar in size to the first one we had built, that cared for dozens of kids and sought our assistance, whether in the form of a partnership or funding, or in the hope that we could take them over as they were on the verge of financial insolvency. As the situation in these homes became more dire we found ourselves receiving more children who simply had nowhere else to go.

In addition to these homes closing their doors, there were families—usually elderly grandparents—who had taken in the grandchildren after the loss of their parents but found themselves unable to continue caring for them. Either through ill health, physical disability or lack of financial means, they simply were unable to provide the ongoing care their kids needed. As the reputation of our home at Baan Tharn Namchai grew within the community, it would become the first place for the local hospital, police and government officials to turn to when they found themselves with a child, sometimes a newborn, without a family. Khun Rotjana found it easier to say yes to giving kids a home than to turn them away.

By 2010 we had committed heavily to Baan Home Hug. We would invest significantly in both building upgrades and infrastructure in addition to the recurrent running costs. In 2011 we opened the community centre that functioned as a tsunami refuge centre, a kindergarten for the local community and a general meeting place for the people of Baan Nam Khem, an area devastated by the tsunami.

In 2011 our responsibilities increased on the back of another tsunami, this one occurring in Japan. While we didn't put money directly into Japan, we did fund two well-established homes at Kanchanaburi and Chumphon that were previously funded in part by Japanese donations. After the 2011 tsunami the money that had been relied on from Japan no longer came and instead remained within the country. An immediate hole existed in the funding of these two homes in Thailand, and *Hands* committed to supporting those homes in the short-term until the funding returned.

Before the end of 2015 we had opened another home, Pama House, in the east of the country at Chanthaburi. We hadn't set out to take on this home or invest in this part of the country; we had more than enough going on, but an Australian doctor had built a home in this region for kids without parents in memory of his parents, whom he had lost at a young age. The home was never completed, and despite his best intentions he was never able to operate the home as intended. To preserve the building and the legacy, we invested in the building and opened it thereafter, providing a safe home for a further 25 kids in need. The restoration and opening of the home at Chanthaburi were made possible by the generosity of Jellis Craig, a Victorian-based real estate company who committed the funds to restore the building and allow for the opening.

In what seemed like a short time I had gone from committing to contributing to the building of one home to having properties across seven different locations with some 350 kids and 70 staff and with a recurrent cost structure of some $1.7 million. Not for the first time I would ask myself *how did we get here?*

Up until the COVID-19 pandemic really impacted us in 2021 we had operated the charity on a structure that saw 100 per cent of donations flow directly to the kids and communities we were supporting in Thailand. Not one cent of donors' money was used in the administration of the charity or on fundraising. We even made deposits into the charity account to ensure the bank fees and international transfer charges were covered. How did we do this, and is it a model charities should aspire to? Let me answer the second question first by saying no! It is a model that worked for us at the time, but I don't claim it offers any kind of gold standard. So how did we make it work?

By 2011 the charity had grown significantly in terms of both our responsibilities and the funds we were raising. Our bike rides had become a permanent fixture in the calendar. It was the first year we had back-to-back rides in January to cater for the demand, and year-on-year growth would continue until 2021. It was also evident that to achieve our potential we needed a bigger support structure in Australia than myself, a volunteer board and a number of other volunteers who committed time when they had it.

The decision of the board was to establish a company that would sit next to the charity. It would be a not-for-profit, meaning no directors or shareholders of the company would profit but it could raise funds through commercial activities rather than through donations. This entity was completely separate from the charity. The company, which became known as Hands Group, generates income in Australia through commercial activities, and those funds allow us to employ staff here in Australia who work to promote and generate further funds on behalf of the charity. Hands Group also meets the fundraising costs of the charity, thereby ensuring the charity dollars raised are 'ring-fenced' for use in Thailand. Hands Group does not receive or handle donations; they are managed by the charity. The company exists to support the efforts of the charity, but the two are different entities.

We rolled into 2020 with a charity that was steadily expanding, enabling us not just to meet the basic needs but to provide university scholarships for kids looking to enter tertiary education. For me, a real measure of our success was our growing number of graduates. It always felt that building the homes, employing the Thai staff, ensuring the kids were fed, healthy and heading to school was the absolute minimum we should aim for.

We were giving the kids a life of choice not chance, enabling them to carve out a future, not just for themselves but for their children, very different from what they would otherwise have had.

If that was all we did with donors' funds I was not convinced we were doing the best we could. But as the number of older kids who entered and then graduated from university grew, it felt as though we were making a measurable difference. We were giving the kids a life of choice not chance, enabling them to carve out a future, not just for themselves but for their children, very different from what they would otherwise have had.

The confidence I have in the difference we have made for the kids rests in no small part on the journeys of two girls who lived with us. Both came to us at a young age. One had lost her parents and relatives during the tsunami; the other was rescued from her father who by any measure had proved unfit to care for her. He lived at the back of a temple in Krabi and was a chronic alcoholic prone to violence when drunk, which was most days of the week, who became more aggressive when he was unable to feed his addiction. He would receive leftover food from the monks, from which he would feed himself and his two daughters. Their hygiene was abysmal, medical care was not an option and school was a place other kids went.

When the neglect of these two girls went from negligent to life-threatening, they were removed and a request was lodged for them to live at Baan Tharn Namchai. How could we say no? The casual observer might argue that they should live with their father, not in a group home, but in reality their father represented the greatest risk to their lives. It was from him they needed saving.

So the girls made Baan Tharn Namchai their home. Their medical needs were attended to, they visited a dentist and they enrolled in school. They loved the comfort of a bed, which wasn't difficult to understand given they had previously slept on the cold cement floor of the temple. The girls started school. They had a long road to make up given how much they had missed, but they did make progress both at school and in the group home. As the years progressed so too did the girls. They formed enduring friendships and demonstrated an appetite for learning. The eldest of the sisters was 15 years of age and had formed an unbreakable friendship with another girl at Baan Tharn Namchai of a similar age.

A tragic accident resulted in the drowning death of the youngest of the two sisters who had lived at the back of the temple. When we returned to Krabi for the funeral I would meet the father of the two girls. On the day of the funeral he was intoxicated when we arrived and as the day wore on he became abusive and threatening. When it came time for us to leave the father physically prevented his eldest daughter from returning to Baan Tharn Namchai. As he remained her legal guardian the staff from BTN had little option and no power to remove her from him. It was Khun Rotjana's opinion that what he saw in his daughter was someone who could work, provide money to buy him alcohol and take care of him.

So the futures of those two 15-year-old girls, the closest of friends, was in all likelihood set in stone that day. The one who returned to BTN would complete high school and go on to study at university, graduating with a degree and with many options open to her. Within 12 months of the funeral, her friend who had returned to the temple in Krabi had given birth to her first child, shortly followed by a second pregnancy. She never returned to school but continued to live in squalid conditions behind the temple, only now she had to care for a child of her own with another on the way.

I could fill the pages of this book with the stories of the kids who came to us. Some of the stories are so horrific you might dismiss them as fiction. I choose not to share those stories to protect the kids. Rather than focus on the past I celebrate the future that we are helping to create for them.

With more than 30 university graduates from across our homes and with exciting plans for the future for the kids for whom university is not a chosen path, I feel we can begin to measure the opportunities we are creating. We can line up the statistics, such as the number of homes we have built, the number of kids we have cared for and the money we have raised. But as impressive as they are, the true measure of our success is twofold: first, the kids we can return to families who are capable of caring for them, and second, for those for whom this is not possible, the futures filled with choice we have opened up for them that might not otherwise have been possible.

WHAT I HAVE LEARNED

If you wait until the time is right to do the things you want to do, that time might never come. At speaking events people will often say to me, I'd love to do what you do, but then list a raft of reasons why they never could. Sometimes we overthink things, persuading ourselves we can't possibly do what we really want to do. We undermine our big ideas with fears and retreat into a state of comfortable inertia.

Building the biggest contributing Australian charity to Thailand was never part of a plan. Raising $30 million wasn't planned either, but it happened. You don't have to have all the answers before you start. You don't even need to know what all the questions are. Sometimes it's as simple as just starting. You can be sure that if you do nothing, then nothing will change.

Focus on the results and not the excuses. There will always be plenty of people who will sit around a table and offer up excuses. Let them worry about the excuses while you focus on the results.

WHAT CAN YOU DO?

What is it that you dream of doing or achieving in the safety of the internal conversations you have with yourself, where you won't be judged, ridiculed or made fun of? Is it learning to dance or to play a musical instrument or starting that business you've always dreamt of? What would happen if you just started? Could it possibly be worse than never starting at all?

CHAPTER 2
MEET UNIQUE CHALLENGES WITH UNIQUE SOLUTIONS

It was while working with Interpol in the counterterrorism community that I first encountered the saying 'hope is not a plan'. We can't just hope that something will or won't happen, but there is only so much contingency planning we can do. When we are presented with unique challenges we need to respond with unique solutions. This is the domain of true leaders who need to develop creative solutions, build teams and confront challenges that haven't been anticipated or planned for.

As the pilot lowered the collective and eased back on the cyclic of his helicopter we commenced the descent, landing in the grounds of the local school. It was the unmistakable smell that confirmed for me that we had arrived at our destination. The smell of death, once experienced, is not something that ever leaves you. For me, it is a legacy of decades of walking into scenes of decomposing bodies and spending hours alone with a lifeless body in a state that is beyond the imagining of most normal people, and for their sake that is a good thing.

Inside the temple at Wat Yan Yao, which had lost the serenity and peace associated with a Buddhist temple and now resembled a gathering of the dead from a horror movie, we were faced with unprecedented and indeed unique challenges. To meet those unique challenges, we needed to find unique solutions.

Our central challenge was and remains the world's largest disaster victim identification attempt ever undertaken. An estimated 250 000 to 300 000 people lost their lives as a result of the Boxing Day tsunami. Given that the movement of tectonic plates occurred off the west coast of Sumatra, it's no surprise that the greatest losses were felt by Indonesia, where almost 228 000 lives were lost. The scale of death in Banda Aceh alone defeated any attempt to undertake the identification process required.

> ## *To meet those unique challenges, we needed to find unique solutions.*

As the tsunami raced across the Indian Ocean it hit the west coast of Thailand, where it claimed 5395 lives. Around half of those were Thai nationals and the remainder were foreign visitors, many of whom were there on holidays over the festive period. I suspect it was the high number of foreign nationals involved that added urgency to the international effort to identify the bodies now laid out in the grounds of Wat Yan Yao.

When the first teams touched down in Thailand the challenges that lay before them hadn't been tested. There was no procedures manual covering what they now faced, no heads of agreement in place between countries addressing who would take charge and how the response should be managed. In chapter 4, I examine the actions of those on the ground and the significance of leading with speed, sensitivity, structure and simplicity. But I have found that the key to bringing clarity to challenging situations is action. The more action you take, the clearer you will become on the solutions required and the direction needed. This is particularly the case in challenging situations where there is no time to plan and rehearse.

The key to bringing clarity to challenging situations is action. The more action you take, the clearer you will become on the solutions required and the direction needed.

Identification after a disaster such as the tsunami or the Bali bombings where the bodies had sustained significant trauma is not, per se, a difficult forensic task. The three main methods of identifying a body are to collect dental, fingerprint or DNA evidence and to compare it with any ante-mortem information that can be collected.

The post-mortem process in Thailand focused solely on identification, rather than cause of death, as would a normal post-mortem. Clothing and jewellery was removed and stored. A forensic odontologist examined the teeth and recorded them via photos and X-rays. A fingerprint expert examined the hands and collected fingerprints using a number of different methods, which is surprisingly achievable even from heavily decomposed bodies. Finally, a sample of bone will be removed for DNA analysis.

In the early days at Wat Yan Yao all of this was undertaken in a makeshift mortuary in the grounds of the temple. With international teams working side by side, it must have felt to most that this was a job without end. For each body examined, a tip truck would arrive at the temple with dozens more.

As this process progressed, police agencies across the globe were flooded with calls from distressed friends and relatives of holiday-makers in Thailand, fearing the worst. The Royal Thai Police were also swamped with calls about lost families from those who had somehow managed to survive. Initially, a missing person report was logged and an investigation commenced. As time passed, and it became increasingly unlikely that the missing person would be found walking down from a mountain top, the second stage of the DVI process began. This involved a more detailed and specific interview based on the presumption that the missing person would show up as one of the thousands of bodies now laid out in the grounds of the temple.

The purpose of the ante-mortem interview is to gather information and physical evidence of the missing person. This will include any dental history gathered from a dentist who had previously treated them. The police will visit the home and collect latent fingerprints and DNA from areas or articles specific to the victim. This might include a hairbrush, toothbrush, or fingerprints from an aftershave or perfume bottle and the like.

We now have a profile of a person, obtained from the body and from their life prior to the event. The forensic specialists will then undertake a comparative analysis, matching the information from the post-mortem and the ante-mortem investigation. Not a complex process for experts in their field—until you have thousands of bodies, tens of thousands of pieces of evidence and thousands upon thousands of computer entries generated.

In laying out the forensic challenge, I have not spoken of the emotional challenges of dealing with such a catastrophe. This emotional challenge is experienced by all involved, though in different ways. The victims' families and friends are in an agony of grief and shock. The foreign nationals must deal with the most confronting and challenging experience of their lives in an unfamiliar country far from home. They had boarded their flight to Thailand filled with excitement and anticipation. Now mothers walk amongst the dead looking for their children, husbands for the wife they had married weeks or decades ago, children struggling to understand why they were alone and when their mum and dad would come back.

If you have ever found yourself ill or injured in another country, or if something else goes seriously wrong while you are travelling, you will probably have felt that overwhelming desire to be home. We feel we can cope better when surrounded by the familiar. How do you navigate the loss of someone dear to you when you don't even speak the native language? What if you have lost multiple members of your family?

Dr Elisabeth Kübler-Ross, a psychiatrist and pioneer of death and dying studies, first developed her groundbreaking model of the five stages of grief in 1969 from her research into those suffering from a terminal illness. She proposed that those they left behind tended to experience all or most of the five stages of adjustment: denial, anger, bargaining, depression and finally acceptance. She suggested that this journey was generally linear: you would pass through each stage in the order presented. However, since her research focused on terminally ill patients it did not necessarily address the impact on those who were exposed to sudden and traumatic loss.

Kübler-Ross acknowledged the limited application of her original conception and later revised it to a seven-stage model: shock, denial, anger, bargaining, depression, testing and acceptance. Shock describes an initial response of emotional paralysis, or numbness, and the testing stage involves trying new ways of coping with loss and rebuilding life after loss.

From my own decades spent dealing with the families of those left behind following a tragic and sudden loss, I can confirm that shock is without question the first overwhelming response.

Of course, the emotions of grief and loss weren't the sole domain of those closely connected or related to the deceased. The forensic specialists who worked in harrowing, heart-wrenching conditions, indeed all of us who travelled across oceans to ply our skills, were experienced in dealing with death, but not on this scale or under these conditions.

For weeks on end every one of us would wake up knowing the kinds of horrors the day ahead had in store. For those of us working with the bodies at Wat Yan Yao or later at Tha Chat Chai, each day involved cracking open the heavy doors of a refrigerated shipping container to be assaulted by a wave of cold air and the smell of death that attached itself to your clothing, and like a beetroot stain on a white t-shirt it never came out. We would search each of the stacked body bags for the attached label that showed the post-mortem number, which represented the provisional identity of the deceased. We would retrieve the bag, remove the badly decomposed body and conduct a post-mortem and return it to the shipping container ... and repeat, endlessly. The knowledge of the tragic circumstances surrounding their deaths was never lost on us. We found ways to mask it so we could work on through each day, but without question it hit us hard, and for many it would have a longer term impact.

Considering the emotional and energy journey our teams went through, I observed a repeating pattern that I have since seen play out in different contexts. What I saw could best be understood as a four-stage cycle, which I called the Crisis Clock. In my experience, this cycle represents what many of us experience when running projects or events—even our bike rides pass through similar stages. I concluded that by understanding those stages, we could better support those experiencing them.

Stage one is the *frantic* stage of a response, and this is where the crisis clock starts ticking. Deployment to Thailand during the tsunami recovery effort was on average for a four-week period. The first week includes travel to Thailand and initiation. It is a time filled with emotion and questions: 'Am I the right person for the job? Do I have the skills required? How will I cope without the language?' The questions don't stop when you arrive—they just change: 'What process and procedures are in place? Who do I report to, and who reports to me?' It's a time full of unknowns and high emotion.

As that first week passes the energy shifts into one that is more productive, generating fewer questions. You are no longer the newest person on the ground. You have a handle on what to do, when to do it—process and order. In my opinion, this is the most productive stage of any project. It is the *controlled* stage. Team members have enough knowledge and energy to deliver at the highest level, unaffected by the impact of having done or seen too much. If they are not motivated at the beginning, you've picked or been given the wrong team.

The third stage of the project (for us, the third week of the deployment) is the most challenging, which is why I call it the *fatigued* stage. Team members are tired of getting up each day to face the same challenges as the day before. The frantic energy of that first week is long gone; the sense of control that marked the second stage has been replaced by a deep weariness. They are missing their families most now, and the end is still a bit too far ahead for them to see the light at the end of the tunnel. This can be the most important stage for a leader. If they are aware of the cycle their teams are going through, if they can be there for their teams through this time, they can bring about significant change to their energy levels and momentum. If you have tricks in your bag to motivate and inspire teams, I suggest it is wasted at the launch of the project. This is when the leader's presence counts most.

If they are not motivated at the beginning, you've picked or been given the wrong team.

Finally, in the *exit* stage, energy levels rise again. The deployment is coming to an end and it's nearly time to head home. You are no longer weighed down by the stressful nature of the work.

There's a good chance you don't work in a crisis or disaster setting and that you or your teams won't be spending weeks at a time surrounded by decomposing bodies. So does the Crisis Clock model offer any broader value? Let me share an example of a context that couldn't be further removed from the forensic work we did after the tsunami.

It is remarkable how neatly the four stages of the Crisis Clock fit into our eight-day charity bike rides. The first two days are absolutely filled with the emotion and energy of the frantic stage. All those questions about their ability, how they will fit in and the 'what ifs'. By the morning of day three they understand the process and that voice in their head that worries about their ability is much quieter. They have found their rhythm and their legs feel strong without tiredness. On top of that, the following day is a rest day, and what's not to look forward to about a rest day?

Day five on the bike normally starts well as you feel rested, have enjoyed a massage and are ready to ride. But if it doesn't hit you by day five, prepare for day six. It is notoriously the hardest day on tour, not because of the length of the day or the elevation you will climb, but because of where it sits within the tour. By now your legs are feeling the punishment, and your bum—well, that won't be getting any better for the rest of the tour. You are probably sick of Thai food and longing for some highly processed carbs. And on the morning of day six you still have a couple of hundred kilometres to ride before the tour is over.

Days seven and eight are pay days. This is when the energy builds again. Day seven is the last full day on the bike and day eight—well, if you're not up for the end of the ride, you shouldn't be on the tour. Energy is high as the finish line is in sight, or at least within a day's ride.

So what can we do with this knowledge of the four stages? Is there some way to move from stage two to stage four and skip the tough days? Well, no, but knowing what's coming and what to expect allows us to prepare and respond wisely.

From a practical point of view, knowing when energy levels will be a bit low in the group, we can be sure to provide some additional food or refreshment to bring a smile to the riders' faces. It might be about saying more or saying nothing at all. The introverts will retreat a little deeper into their cave, and giving them the space to ride on on their own can be sufficient. I'd like to claim that I have the emotional intelligence to manage my own energy through day six, but knowing what's happening doesn't necessarily mean I can avoid it. It does, however, mean I can identify it for what it is and allow it to pass, which it does.

On a recent tour, one of the riders didn't look all that happy with life. 'How're you travelling?' I asked, and her response summed up day six well: 'I'm going to sit in the van and sulk for the next leg.' And she did, but by the end of the next leg she was back on her bike, done with the sulking and ready to move forward. There was nothing more to it, just a case of day six giving her the shits!

As leaders, so much of our job is looking after those around us. It's about making their time interesting, rewarding, something they feel connected to. As Simon Sinek says, 'When we work hard for something we don't believe in, it's called stress. When we work hard for something we love, it's called passion.'

Working in a crisis and disaster setting there is a role for command-and-control leadership. Decisions need to be made fast, and making difficult decisions then living with the outcome is the role and responsibility of leaders. Leaders who lead successfully during times of crisis enjoy the trust of their teams, a trust that has usually been established long before the crisis response. They believe their leaders are operating in the best interest of the team and not just seeking to advance their personal cause or profile.

Having worked in crisis and disaster situations around the globe I have witnessed first-hand many good, great and reluctant leaders, and learned from all of them.

Leaders who lead successfully during times of crisis enjoy the trust of their teams, a trust that has usually been established long before the crisis response.

Working in a specialist area of the police, we thought that our skills and roles were unique and best understood by those who had spent their careers working in the area. But what I have come to learn after working with all types of industries is that the role of leaders is not all that different no matter what industry you are in. The further you move away from the technical side of the job, the more your role is about supporting those with the technical skill, regardless of the industry you're in.

We used to have a saying that you would be promoted until you reached your level of incompetence, and for some that came more quickly than for others. But it really is less about the ability of the individual than about how we prepare and train our leaders for their leadership roles.

Whether you are an accountant, a surgeon, a builder or a butcher, it takes years of study and/or practice to become proficient in your craft. When I trained as a crime scene specialist, it took me countless hours of study at university and an equal number of hours completing internal courses and proficiency tests to qualify as a forensic specialist and be accepted as an expert whose opinion-based evidence could be depended on in court. You, and perhaps your organisation, will need to make an investment of five to ten years or longer to reach that level of a competent practitioner. Combine a high level of technical skill with experience and you can expect to be promoted above the level of practitioner to someone who is responsible for those doing the job you were really good at. So you transition from doing the job to supporting those doing the job. This is where good leaders thrive.

We've invested all this time in developing the technical competence needed to do the job, and those who do it best are commonly rewarded by being promoted out of the role. Most often there hasn't been an investment in upskilling them as future leaders, because until they won the promotion they weren't identified as such. The successful leader will accept that their role is now to support those doing the job they used to do so well.

Those who struggle to step into the leadership role will revert to what they know—the technical skills—and then micromanage those now doing the job. Lacking the competence to lead, their skills continue to lie in the technical role.

Great leaders I have worked with make this transition well. They accept they are no longer responsible for doing the job; they are responsible for those doing the job. As Dr Max Goodwin in the TV drama *New Amsterdam* continually asks his hospital team, 'How can I help?'

Something we need to acknowledge is that while we all have the capacity to lead, we may not have the necessary desire. Forcing someone into a leadership position against their will is likely to result in ineffective leadership and a lack of incisive decision making. Someone may choose not to take a leadership role for various reasons, including a reluctance to take on the increased responsibility or time commitment required. Or perhaps the desire is there but the culture of the organisation is such that the prospect of the increased pressure serves as a disincentive.

Cultural traits of an organisation or even a country that may deter a prospective leader from stepping up can include a punitive culture where people are censured or even penalised for their mistakes, or the leader is held accountable for group failure. In Thailand, for example, there can be a very real reluctance in highly competent individuals to pursue leadership roles for fear of the consequences should their decisions or those of the group they lead be found wanting. For many the risk is far greater than the reward, and they are happy to sit back and let others lead.

The hotel and hospitality sector offers a very visible example of this problem. Many of the larger, best-known branded hotels have senior leaders who were born outside of Thailand. For most hotels, it is not their desire that the hotel general managers be from outside the country; rather, it is that they struggle to attract Thai nationals into the very senior and demanding positions. It may well come down to a question of trust and competence. The potential leaders have the necessary competence, but they don't trust the owners of the hotels to tolerate their making mistakes without attracting punishment.

For many the risk is far greater than the reward, and they are happy to sit back and let others lead.

Additional reasons for not taking positions of leadership may include environments where a leadership role is offered without additional support, training or mentoring, or where an increase in expectations and responsibility is not matched by the remuneration or reward offered.

Further considerations are a belief in the vision of the organisation and a trust in the leader above them. When we invest more, which is what is required when taking on a more responsible leadership position, we need clarity around what will be expected of us, what we are aiming to achieve, what strategic direction we will take and how our success or failure will be measured. Without clarity about those overarching issues, how do we lead our team?

If there has previously been a high turnover among those in leadership positions, or your new direct report has a poor reputation in leading those under them, the reward offered is unlikely to compensate for the rocky road ahead. You'll want to feel you have the trust and support you need and will be mentored into the role, especially if you're feeling you are not good enough for the role on offer and that there are better candidates out there.

In times of crisis and disaster true leaders are identified by their actions and reactions. It is less about their position or title and more about what they do. Following the deadly floods in the city of Jeddah in Saudi Arabia, my work was twofold—first, to review the response to the disaster in which 122 people died and to look for systemic issues that might have contributed; and then to provide advice around crisis prevention, mitigation and leadership during future disasters.

Focusing solely on the response to the crisis, as opposed to the cause, it was clear to me that a lack of leadership resulted in a higher death count than might otherwise have occurred. The response was multi-jurisdictional but was confined to agencies within the country. However, the lack of coordination and of clear leadership exacerbated the problems. Many of the responding agencies acted without central coordination and without a clear leadership structure. While varying agencies vied for overall control time was wasted, and people died as a result.

> *The leader's role is to inspire and motivate, to set the course and lead towards vision and change.*

By contrast, in the international response in Thailand following the Boxing Day tsunami, which involved teams from 36 different countries, the leadership structure formed smoothly, logically and without challenge. It was based on what each team did once they arrived into Thailand, not the positions they held in their respective countries prior to flying out, which were no longer relevant once on the ground.

Unique challenges require unique solutions. The manager's role is to follow process and ensure the effective use of resources with a focus on the delivery of tasks. The leader's role is to inspire and motivate, to set the course and lead towards vision and change. We want our leaders to be creative and courageous, to be innovative and to inspire those around them.

WHAT I HAVE LEARNED

The bigger the challenge, the greater the opportunity to lead. It is not the loudest or the biggest personality who will be the best leader, it is the one who is truly there for their people and has the courage to make difficult decisions. They will accept responsibility for their mistakes and those of the team they lead. They will not cast blame on those whose decisions prove to be ill-advised. They will look to support and elevate those around them.

Ability doesn't necessarily mean desire, and equally desire doesn't mean ability. My experience through participation and observation has taught me that good people who express a desire to take leadership roles balanced with a degree of self-reflection and a genuine ambition to help those around them are likely to make great leaders.

Considering our own personal leadership challenges and opportunities, what is certain is that we don't have to have all the answers. We don't even have to know what the questions are going to be. With action comes clarity. If we continue to ask 'How can I help?' with a view of elevating those around us, we are on the path to successful leadership.

WHAT CAN YOU DO?

Consider the leaders around you who either have a direct or indirect impact on you. They may be in your own workplace or someone who holds an elected office, a community leader or the coach of the kids' soccer team. Think about what it is about their leadership style that you most admire or dislike. Remember, you can draw valuable lessons to assist you when facing your own unique leadership challenges from both positive and negative role models.

When faced with what seems like an insurmountable challenge or problem, remember to start small and scale the solution.

CHAPTER 3
EMBRACE COURAGEOUS LEADERSHIP

Leadership is about making difficult decisions and then living with the outcome. It is not about avoiding responsibility or passing it on to someone else. True leaders have the courage to make the tough decisions. If we make our decisions with integrity and good intent, consulting where circumstances allow, and we still make the wrong decision, we will be forgiven. Failing to make difficult decisions for fear of getting it wrong shows a lack of courage and undermines trust in those around you. By failing to make a decision you are putting your interests before the cause. You're saying you would rather not be seen to be wrong than make the tough decision.

Some decisions will define you and live with you for the rest of your life.

Little boys love to run fast, real fast. Aek was in the race of his life, or to be more accurate it was a race *for* his life. He held his grandfather's hand and they were running from the tsunami. Fifty metres in front of them was a building and if they could reach that building they would have a chance of survival. But run as fast they might, they knew they were never going to be able to outrun that wall of water.

So when Granddad reached the base of a tree he climbed that tree dragging little Aek up with him, and they made it to the top of the tree. They were bruised, scratched and bleeding, but they had survived. They felt no cause for celebration, though. You see, while Granddad clutched Aek in his right hand, in his left he held the hand of Aek's younger brother.

When he got to the base of the tree he knew that if he didn't survive none of them would. Neither of his grandchildren stood a chance without him. But he also knew he couldn't climb the tree hanging onto both of them. He had a decision to make: which of his grandchildren would he hold onto and which would he let go of?

How do you make that kind of decision? How do you decide who lives and who dies? He had only seconds, but all the minutes that make up a year wouldn't be enough to reconcile such a decision.

The old man let go of Aek's younger brother and he was washed away. The little boy died that day.

For years I would see Aek's grandfather whenever I returned to Thailand. The decision he was forced to make that day broke him. He was haunted by three questions: 'Could I have run faster? Could I have been stronger? Could I have made a different decision?'

But what was the right decision if not the one he made? Who among us could imagine being in a similar situation and making the 'right' choice? 'Right' for whom? To my mind Aek's grandfather showed enormous courage in making a difficult (even impossible) decision. That's what real leadership is about.

All of us will be faced with difficult decisions on both a personal and a professional level. For those with higher levels of responsibility those decisions are likely to impact a greater number of people and therefore carry with them a greater burden of responsibility. For the more difficult decisions we will lie awake for hours on end worrying over the best course to take. We'll make the decision and then spend more sleepless nights stewing over whether the decision was the 'right' one. But this is where we should take comfort in making difficult decisions because that is the responsibility of leaders.

I haven't seen Aek's grandfather for many years now. I suspect he's no longer with us. I hadn't known him prior to the tsunami, but I think it likely that his fateful decision that day affected him so deeply that it had a profound impact on his soul. His burden, I believe, was a heartbreak from which he never recovered.

In the 20 years since I met Aek and his grandfather I have thought of them often. It is a story I share because I believe it offers an incredibly powerful message about our need to accept the difficult decisions we're forced to make and find peace in the outcome. I think about how he might have made the decision. Perhaps it was the child in his weakest hand he let go of for fear of dropping him, or was he freeing up his strongest hand for the climb? I don't imagine there was the time to contemplate which of them deserved the greater chance to live.

But what of the years that followed, when he challenged himself so relentlessly? Did he find a way to play it out so all three of them, or at least the children, survived? I imagine that was the story he told himself over and over again. 'What if ...?' But we don't always get second chances when making the tough decisions. We don't have the opportunity to build a working group to consider the pros and cons, or to run a blind survey to determine the best option.

This is the harsh reality for leaders who are forced to make difficult decisions. Mercifully, for most of us they are not often about who will live and who will die, though later in this book I share the story of Mae Thiew, who had to do just this on a weekly basis, when she had to decide who should receive the medicine and who should not, knowing that whatever she did with what she had it was never going to be enough, and children would die. I am intrigued and inspired by how she continued for so many years.

We don't always get second chances when making the tough decisions. We don't have the opportunity to build a working group to consider the pros and cons, or to run a blind survey to determine the best option.

There aren't many occupations where it is part of the job to decide who lives and who dies. Those responsible for allocating organs for transplant come to mind, as do those working in field hospitals among the sickest on Earth and medical staff in wartime who must judge who has the better chance of survival. But for the vast majority of us making such fateful decisions is not something we expect to do walking out the door each day. So how does courageous leadership impact us and what does it look like?

To make difficult, courageous decisions whose impact will reverberate across time, find your true north—the goal towards which you are working. You need clarity of purpose around the fundamental thing that is most important to you and to the organisation. What are the absolute non-negotiables? Being clear as an individual and as a business makes the decision-making process so much easier. Clarity of purpose helps us make difficult decisions and live with the outcomes; it allows us to be courageous leaders.

So what is my clarity of purpose? When joining the NSW Police the idea of working internationally was never on the cards. It was just not something that was even remotely foreseeable. If you wanted the chance to work internationally you joined the Australian Federal Police. My work in Bali after the bombings changed all that.

Clarity of purpose helps us make difficult decisions and live with the outcomes; it allows us to be courageous leaders.

From a leadership perspective, my knowledge and expertise in the area of forensic science, and in particular disaster victim identification, made it a near certainty that if there was a large-scale disaster in the Indo-Pacific region I would likely be called upon to assist. The Boxing Day tsunami triggered such a call-up.

At the time of the tsunami I was on holiday with my family on the south coast of New South Wales. As the news broke it became clear that we would deploy to Thailand and it was a matter of days after the event that I left for Thailand. It was my first visit to the country and I had no notion of the impact it would have on my life.

Eventually I would undertake multiple rotations, each several weeks long. Before leaving on my final tour, Jack, my youngest son, then aged seven, said to me, 'Dad, please don't go. We miss you when you're gone. Why do you have to go?' I was then leading the Australian team on deployment in addition to one of the international sites. It was a great honour and I was humbled that it had been entrusted to me, but that wasn't why I was going.

I took my three kids and sat them down and said to them, 'On Boxing Day there were families just like us, mum, dad and the kids, on the beach all having a wonderful time. It was 10 o'clock in the morning when the water went out and stayed out for a long time.' I told my kids how this strange event brought more people down to the water's edge. They didn't know what was happening. Then the water came back in, and when it did so it was in the form of a solid wall of water that was 10 metres high, and it came so fast people couldn't outrun it.

'Among the families on the beach that day, some kids escaped, some mums and dads made it, but very few families survived intact. It was a miracle that kids survived when their parents didn't. But those kids now found themselves alone without their parents, some of them in a foreign country. How scared must they have been! The foreign kids from all over the world remained in Thailand until someone helped them return to their own country. They went home to mourn and to try to make sense of their life now. But where would these kids go on Mother's Day to lay some flowers for their lost mum? Where would they go on Dad's birthday to share some stories, because until their bodies were identified their loved ones would stay in Thailand. It could take weeks or months for us to identify and return them.'

For those of you who have children in your life, and most of us do, whether they are your own kids or stepkids, nieces or nephews, or grandchildren, imagine this. You are on that beach with your children and you see that impossible wall of water coming in. You grab your kids and you run, but the wall catches up with you. It knocks you over and you fight it with all your strength, and for some reason you survive ... but your children are gone. You search for them desperately, go to all the hospitals, the victim centres, the temples. But there comes a point when you can no longer remain in Thailand and must return home without that most precious thing in your life — your kids.

How can you possibly move forward, without answers? You spend your days hoping that someone like me will call you and say, 'It's okay, we found them, and they're alive.' Common sense tells you that's not going to happen, that your children have died. But how can you possibly move forward? 'This is why I have to go back,' I told my kids. I help identify mums and dads and kids and bring them home.

I have never personally known the grief so many families suffered as a result of the tragic events on December 26, 2004, though my professional career has afforded me a window into the lives of those who have suffered such loss. What I know is that the loss is compounded many times over when the body of their loved one isn't recovered and returned to them to allow a ceremony according to their faith and their beliefs.

A difficult day working in Thailand was rarely the result of one thing in particular; it was more often the build-up of emotion, the enormity of what lay before us. It then became especially important for us to understand why we did what we did. For me this was encapsulated by Alexander. He was 18 months old, was from Sweden and was lost by his family. I saw his identification and the return of his body to his family as the reason I was there. Alexander represented for me the 5395 bodies lost by their families, and I saw my role in Thailand to provide his family with answers.

Having our own reasons for being there enabled each of the forensic staff on deployment from other lands to answer their own 'why' during those challenging times. You couldn't spend weeks that stretched into months doing what we did without difficult times, and I know for some those difficult times didn't end when they left Thailand.

Thought leader Simon Sinek first identified the power of 'starting with why': determining why we do what we do. What is our purpose? Sinek believes, '"Why" is probably the most important message that an organization or individual can communicate as this is what inspires others to action.' He explains, 'Very few organisations know why they do what they do. Why is not about making money. That's a result. Why is a purpose, a cause or belief. It is the very reason your organization exists.'

Providing answers became most important to me and answered the question I asked of myself and others asked of me around why I was doing this work. When I was a crime scene investigator, my role wasn't to secure convictions but to provide answers to questions for the jury and those who sat in judgement. While the questions have changed, providing answers has continued to motivate me over the past two decades in my work with *Hands*. The answers we provide are to the questions of the safety, health and education of the kids. We are there to provide solutions to these big questions.

Asking why is as important for businesses as it is for individuals. A business might engage consultants and spend days on an off-site composing the company's values and vision statements. The more successful companies are often those where there is the greatest congruence between the actions of the leaders, the teams they support and their stated values.

As individuals we don't necessarily hang our values on the living-room wall, but a clear sense of purpose underwrites the values we hold ourselves accountable for. Whatever is most important to us on a deep level guides us when it comes to making the tough decisions that courageous leaders need to make.

Courageous leaders lead with humility, admit to their weaknesses and openly acknowledge mistakes when they get it wrong. The courage to be vulnerable is a strength we admire in our leaders today.

They canvass the views of others, actively listen and seek out alternative opinions before making decisions.

As individuals we don't necessarily hang our values on the living-room wall, but a clear sense of purpose underwrites the values we hold ourselves accountable for.

When I consider leaders whom I have worked with and admired, each of them has demonstrated remarkable courage. A number of consistent traits stand out in my mind.

They are authentic in how they present themselves. That authenticity breeds trust and commitment from those they work with or influence. Leadership is a tough gig and can be lonely. Courageous leaders demonstrate resilience and self-care. To lead with courage, they need to embrace uncertainty and not be afraid of failure—and when they do fail, they own it. Living a courageous life means seldom taking the easy path. They make difficult decisions not without fear but in spite of it. And they create a safe space for those around them.

To lead with courage, they need to embrace uncertainty and not be afraid of failure—and when they do fail, they own it.

If we agree that creating a safe space for others is one role of a courageous leader then part of that role will be to address the behaviour of others who infringe on that safe space.

A courageous leader also considers how their own personal views, feelings and actions might impact others. For me, one memorable encounter exemplified such leadership.

A part of my job at Tha Chat Chai was to oversee the return of the identified bodies to their family if they were Thai nationals or their repatriation to their own country if they were foreign nationals. In the case of foreign nationals, a police representative from that country would come to our site to receive the body and would then facilitate the return home to their loved ones for burial or cremation. If it was a Thai national, members of the family would come to our site to receive the body, which was usually then transported to their temple, often located back in the village where they had grown up, for cremation. For some this was a journey of hundreds of kilometres.

One day I met a Thai woman who had travelled from an area six hours north to collect the body of her son. She arrived in a beat-up utility and it was clear that she came from incredibly modest circumstances. She arrived without a coffin, which meant she would receive her son in a body bag, which would have to be carried in the back of the open ute for the six-hour drive back to her village. We had been caught out by this scenario once before, and once was enough. We agreed then and there that this would never occur again. No parent, no matter who they were, should collect the body of their child in this undignified manner. So we purchased a number of very basic coffins that could be provided to the families who were receiving and transporting their loved one often considerable distances back to their home village.

When this beautiful Thai woman arrived she had to be at the lowest point of her life. We provided her with the body of her son and a coffin to carry him home in. Despite her own personal grief and sorrow, all she could do was thank us for the work we had done. She demonstrated more grace, dignity and compassion than anyone I had ever met. She didn't pretend she wasn't grieving or broken inside, but she still showed care and compassion for those around her. That is true courage.

One thing we know, though, is that the world is not necessarily a fair place and for some it can be cruel. You see, I didn't meet this woman just once. She didn't make that 12-hour journey to us on just one occasion, or even twice. Three times she would visit our site to collect the bodies of her three children, all of whom perished in the tsunami. But each time she came she showed the same grace, dignity and compassion. And each time I felt incredibly bad that I couldn't do more for her than return her dead children. I could see the pain and heartbreak. I could see how her soul ached from her loss, but still she didn't project her pain onto us. In spite of such unfathomable loss she still considered us and expressed her gratitude for the work we were doing.

She didn't pretend she wasn't grieving or broken inside, but she still showed care and compassion for those around her. That is true courage.

It probably comes as no surprise that when I think about the quality of courage I think of Mae Thiew. While her journey is very different from that of the woman who visited our site at Tha Chat Chai to collect the bodies of her three children, the attributes they share are remarkable. When I think of Mae Thiew it is of her resilience, her authenticity and her ability to sustain a life of uncertainty in a way I believe few could match. The resilience she demonstrated in the face of such adversity is unparalleled in my experience. There is no escape for her. She doesn't get to go home and decompress and return the next day. There are no holidays away from her home without the kids. There can be no respite from her loss. But she endures, and I believe a massive part of that is her connection to purpose, why she does what she does, her ability to focus on tomorrow and move on quickly from yesterday.

As you will learn through the pages of this book, Mae Thiew has become not only a source of inspiration to me and those who have spent time with her, but a close and trusted friend whose company I enjoy every chance I get. She has ridden many times with us on our 800 km bike rides. They were easier for her when her health was better, but her presence always draws people to her, like moths to a flame. She speaks quietly and chooses her words carefully. Her English is sufficient to allow us to engage in conversations that last for hours. She is fluent in English until she chooses not to be, based on her audience. She possesses a gravitas that speaks to the authenticity she brings to each and every interaction. When she speaks her mind (sometimes in a most un-Thai-like way), she is very clear and transparent and calls out those she believes are acting without pure intent. She doesn't seek confrontation, but she won't back away from it either, which is again unusual among Thais.

For us, her company is especially refreshing in a country where you can leave an hour-long conversation with no clear idea of a person's feelings or any agreement reached. Given a desire not to offend, this can be confusing to say the least.

The late James Baldwin wrote, 'Not everything that is faced can be changed, but nothing can be changed until it is faced.' Courageous leaders turn up and face the challenges of our times.

WHAT I HAVE LEARNED

Reflecting on the leaders I have worked with or observed over many years, the courageous leaders are often not the loud, domineering ones who make a lot of noise and call attention to themselves or their actions. Rather, they go about their business quietly but with clarity of purpose and direction. They are willing to make the difficult decisions, which are not always the popular ones, and are happy to take the fall when things don't pan out. They don't throw people under the bus to save themselves or their image, and they seek out opportunities to lift others up, often at their own expense.

We value courageous leaders because they value us, and this builds trust. We are drawn to them not because they have all the answers, but because when they don't they acknowledge that and seek our input.

WHAT CAN YOU DO?

Courageous leaders aren't born so; it's something they become. You need to work constantly on your own development. Building the traits of a courageous leader needs constant work and practice. Learn to confront your fears and move forward in spite of them. You'll find that this becomes easier the more you do it. Remain current and informed, and invest in your own self-care.

Study the models around you. Who in your world do you admire for their conviction, their willingness to put others ahead of their own self-interest and to demonstrate resilience and resolve, particularly in difficult times? When you find them, lean in a little closer.

CHAPTER 4

BE PRESENT AND SHOW YOU CARE

In my experience of working in crisis and disaster settings, true leaders are identified by their actions and reactions. It's what people do that matters, not their position or title. I call this leadership without authority. As leaders, we don't have to be implementing change all the time. We do have to demonstrate that we care and that we understand. Presence gives you both insight and understanding.

This was clearly evident in the role the Australians played when deployed to Thailand after the Boxing Day tsunami. No conditions had been imposed on the Thais by the Australian Government, but something interesting happened after the Australians landed and found their way to the temple at Wat Yan Yao. In the days, weeks and months that followed the Australians would hold many of the key leadership positions in the international response.

It's worth considering why the Australians came to hold those leadership positions. We didn't arrive first, we didn't have any greater skills or experience, we didn't have access to resources other countries did not, and we certainly didn't lose more people than other countries. Quite the contrary. We lost 26 people. Germany and Sweden both lost 500, and 2500 Thais were lost. So what was it that put the Australians into those positions of leadership?

> *It's what people do that matters, not their position or title. I call this leadership without authority.*

I think there were four key things the Australians did well from day one that thrust us into those leadership positions.

First, we acted with speed. Not with reckless haste, but by taking prompt, decisive and considered actions. If you wait until you have all the answers to all the possible questions you may never move forward. When there is a gap in the market, whatever marketplace you operate in, if you wait too long before you take action to fill that gap, the one certain thing is that one of your competitors will step forward and seize the opportunity.

> *First, we acted with speed. Not with reckless haste, but by taking prompt, decisive and considered actions. If you wait until you have all the answers to all the possible questions, you may never move forward.*

Think of the global taxi industry and the holiday accommodation market in recent years. Is the market dominance now enjoyed by Uber and Airbnb due to their offering the best service for their customers? Are they the sole operator in their space? I think we can find plenty of evidence to answer in the negative to both questions. So why do they enjoy such market dominance? Because they were the first to move, the first to offer an alternative service. No matter what ride service app you use, you'll likely speak of 'booking an Uber'. It's not because they are necessarily the best, cheapest or fastest; it's because they moved first to fill a gap in the marketplace we didn't even know existed.

This is what happened in Thailand. Ultimately, more than 450 forensic staff from 36 different countries would travel to Thailand. There was no overall leadership structure in place. No one had ever considered a response on this scale, with this many different specialists from so many countries participating. Arriving in Thailand in the early days following the tsunami, my read on what happened is that whoever moved first and demonstrated leadership by their actions would in all likelihood position themselves as the leading authority. Rather than being predetermined, the structure was a result of actions and reactions. Those first Australian police and forensic specialists showed the way, demonstrating knowledge and taking action, and people followed their lead.

There was nothing special about what was done, nothing the Australians did that the French, Germans or British couldn't have done. We weren't the best. We held the positions of authority and leadership simply because we moved first.

The second thing the Australian leaders did well was lead with sensitivity when dealing with change. More often than not change programs we lead or are part of are met with resistance. Seldom is a new change program met with enthusiasm by anyone other than the author of the change process, who naturally believes it's a great idea.

Author and speaker Seth Godin has a habit of making sense of things. In relation to change he has said, 'If you're not upsetting people you're not changing the status quo.' If we are going to lead a change program, there's a good chance we're going to upset people. That shouldn't be a surprise, but how often do we seek to address the issues of resistance *before* implementing our change program?

We weren't the best. We held the positions of authority and leadership simply because we moved first.

After the Bali bombings in 2002, the bodies of those who died were taken to Sanglah Hospital in Denpasar. The mortuary had a capacity for six; the bombings produced 202 victims, many of whose bodies were not intact due to the extreme trauma they had suffered. As the number of bodies overwhelmed the capacity of the mortuary, they were placed on the ground on the walkways between hospital wards and covered with ice in an effort to slow decomposition, which is accelerated by heat.

In those early days family members and travelling companions of the missing wandered through the hospital looking for lost friends and loved ones. Because, make no mistake, if you were caught up in a similar disaster while holidaying in a foreign country with family or friends, you would not rest until you had found them and taken them home. No one willingly leaves their loved ones behind.

Many victims of the tsunami in southern Thailand were initially taken to a beautiful temple called Wat Yan Yao. This temple is located north of the major tourist destination of Khao Lak, which is approximately 150 km north of Phuket International Airport.

Bodies were brought to the temple quite literally by the truckload, and there were no facilities to store them so they were lined up on the ground within the confines of the temple. Again, family members had to thread their way between the rows of bodies in various stages of decomposition in search of those they had lost.

It was a harrowing sight that those who witnessed it will never forget, the horror only compounded by the distress of the hundreds of relatives who arrived each day to search for their children, husbands, wives and parents. Many would spend hours searching in vain, to leave without answers but in increased anguish.

I met one woman who had spent three days amongst the thousands of bodies at the temple searching for the body of her seven-year-old daughter. Finally, at the end of the third day she came across the body of a young girl and told the Thai police on site, 'This is my daughter.' Asked if she was sure, she replied, 'Without hesitation.' So they allowed her to take the body, classifying it as a 'visual identification'. Tragically, it would prove not to be the body of her daughter at all. Cremating the body of what she suspected was her daughter meant that another family had now had that right taken away from them.

On a professional level, I have found only one conversation more difficult than informing a family that their child is dead, and that is to explain to a family that, yes, their daughter is dead, she has been identified, but her body has been mistakenly taken and cremated by someone else. For the life of me, I can't imagine how you could recover from that.

Such a mistake cannot be undone, and to prevent it happening again there had to be a change to the process. Our challenge in the early days in Thailand was to impose standards, practices and procedures that were unfamiliar in that country. It was a significant, essential change that needed to occur, and to bring about such change the coroner, police and other parties needed to be in agreement. The reason the change was successfully negotiated, in my opinion, was because the areas of resistance were identified and addressed prior to attempting to bring about the change. The change process was led with a degree of sensitivity that acknowledged the different parties involved and the importance of achieving the desired outcome.

As much as I may sometimes resist operating within a formal structure, I am the first to acknowledge that it drives consistency, predictability and order in our operations. And I'm thankful that many in my circle enjoy process and a good spreadsheet, even though I don't!

Given the scale of the disaster, the operation in Thailand was only ever going to be successful if it relied on an agreed process. The process we established was one that was universally accepted by police agencies across the world for mass disaster events. As I have noted, mistakes in this environment cannot easily be undone. We needed structure and we needed consistency.

But here's the thing: the more structure we entrench, the more we take away from our leaders. When we implement policy and procedures, we reduce innovation and the creativity and decision-making skills of our team. We weaken that decision-making muscle, so when situations arise outside of the policy and procedures, we have disempowered our teams to make creative decisions with confidence. The intent of policy and procedure is to be able to predict outcomes, but the more structure we put in place, the more likelihood there is of non-compliance.

One of the things the police were good at was holding reviews or debriefs into operations. The bigger the operation, the bigger the review and the more people involved in it. A large review seldom concluded that 'we have enough in place around policy, no need for more'. When a review was conducted and gaps were found, a team would come together to fill that gap with more policy and more procedure. But when the review was conducted and *no* gaps were found, they would still want to initiate new policy and procedure, and then they'd be surprised by the emergence of a culture of not making decisions for fear of breaching the plethora of policy that existed.

The intent of policy and procedure is to predict outcomes, but the more structure we put in place, the more likelihood there is of non-compliance.

The more structure you implement, the more policy you write and the greater your chance of killing the creativity of your team and taking away their true leadership abilities.

Australia's productivity is being choked by red tape, with the combined cost of administering and complying with public- and private-sector bureaucracy costing the nation $250 billion every year.

Strikingly, the cost of complying with self-imposed rules created by the private sector is double that associated with government regulations, according to Deloitte Access Economics. The self-imposed rules of the private sector cost $155 billion a year: $21 billion to develop and administer, and a stunning $134 billion a year in compliance costs.

Deloitte's report, 'Get out of your own way: Unleashing productivity', identifies the costs to corporates and the nation of self-imposed red tape. It shows that the time required for employees to comply with self-imposed rules has become a crippling burden. Middle managers and senior executives chalk up 8.9 hours a week complying with the rules that firms set for themselves, with other staff spending 6.4 hours.

The report acknowledges the need for regulation and control but it also notes the business trend of 'reaching for rules'. We have created a seriously large industry, the cost of which has to be passed on to the goods and services we consume, to tell people how to do things, provide them with rules and check they are complying with them.

I once sat in the auditorium listening to a lecture on the implementation of accreditation in our forensic laboratories and the compliance of our practices with ISO standards. I remember it as clearly as if it was yesterday. We were embarking on the accreditation of our systems and processes, which would be a way of demonstrating that we did what we said we did.

'My advice to you is to keep the processes simple.' This from the people at the National Association of Testing Authorities whose job it was to oversee and advise on our accreditation. 'Don't overcomplicate it,' they told us. Did those whose very jobs revolved around the implementation of accreditation keep it simple? Of course they didn't. In some strange way, it was almost as though the more complicated the systems and procedures, the more their role was justified.

The effect of overcomplicating the standards we were putting in place was to lead to more opportunities for non-compliance and to take away opportunities for decision making, which is okay when you are working with constants. But in undefined, uncertain and ever-shifting environments we need at least our leaders, if not all our people, to be encouraged to exercise diligence and to make analytical decisions in response to changing circumstances. If we train our teams and leaders merely to follow process we are taking away their creative thinking skills. What we are hoping for is that when the authors of the process and policies have sat around workshopping how things should be done, according to them, they have considered every conceivable variable.

What I admired most about the leaders I worked with and alongside during my various international deployments was their ability and willingness to make decisions when necessary. I never felt they were reckless or ill-considered in their approach. They backed their expertise and recognised that in times of crisis and disaster many ongoing decisions are needed, and they are needed without a steering committee to hide behind.

Those first leaders on the ground created the blueprint for the operation and by taking action early on, leading with sensitivity and simplicity.

The policing environment is paradoxical on decision making. On one hand you have courageous men and women making literally life-defining decisions with split seconds to consider the consequences; on the other, a rigid hierarchy that breeds a culture of sending decisions up the line. As a leader, reports frequently hit your desk seeking a decision, and more often than not your first response is to append the note 'forwarded for advice or consideration' and simply pass the buck upwards, avoiding responsibility. If it's easier to defer, why would you do otherwise. Based on my experience, I have no doubt the culture of passing up the line was encouraged by the imposition of excessive structure, as discussed in the previous section. As more and more structure was put in place, more and more policy existed, the risks of offending some policy encouraged a culture of deference.

What I witnessed in Thailand from so many of the leaders who represented both the Australian Federal Police and the state jurisdictions who deployed resources to support the AFP was courage in decision making. Those first leaders on the ground created the blueprint for the operation and by taking action early on, leading with sensitivity and simplicity, set future Australian representatives up with an inherent level of credibility.

Policies and structures for how to identify the bodies existed, but—and this might sound strange—that was the easy part. As I have mentioned, identification through forensic science is not complex; it was the volume that created the complexity. For this scale of disaster there were no rules written, no precedent to fall back on, which meant some decisions could be made with speed and progress made at a pace that without question gave comfort to the grieving families.

I have discussed in some detail the four key components of what I witnessed and was part of in the early days in Thailand. That first six weeks was when the biggest change took place and the foundations were laid for the following 10 months. But on reflection, years later, I believe there was something that was even more important than acting with speed, sensitivity, having a structure and leading with simplicity. It was the *presence* of the leaders.

The value of presence occurred to me while standing in a small community hall in Iwate Prefecture, Japan, in early 2011. It was the aftermath of the tsunami that devastated so much of the east coast of that beautiful country and claimed close to 20 000 lives. Once again I found myself in a foreign country, one that I would come to love, walking through the devastation, the enormity of which I had never seen before. Travelling through the ravaged region, visiting and meeting with locals and community leaders, it was heartbreaking to see the human losses and the destruction of temples that had stood for hundreds of years.

Mr Sato Sun was a community leader from a small fishing village that like many up and down the coast had experienced great destruction and loss of life. I had been invited to the community hall, which served as the meal centre for those who had lost their homes. Each night they gathered in this small hall for their meal, where Mr Sato joined them, as he had done every evening since the first meal was served. The thing was Mr Sato's house had not been destroyed; he had not sustained any loss as his house was on a hill safely above the rising waters. But as a community leader he joined those who had suffered to share in their loss and to demonstrate by his presence that he cared and that he understood their loss.

He didn't have the answers. He couldn't immediately solve their problems, but through his presence he could convey hope to those who had little.

He didn't need to be there to understand the infrastructure challenges that lay ahead for the community. He wasn't gathering otherwise unobtainable information. What he was doing was demonstrating to those who needed to know that people cared. He didn't have the answers. He couldn't immediately solve their problems, but through his presence he could convey hope to those who had little.

Think about significant events at a global and local level and look for evidence of the importance of presence.

Closer to home, we can draw lessons from leaders in times of crisis whose actions have defined their legacy.

Christine Nixon was the Chief Commissioner of the Victorian Police at the time of the Black Saturday bushfires in Victoria in February 2009, in which 173 people lost their lives. Nixon was criticised for her absence on the day of the greatest loss of life, when she had left the command centre to fulfil a number of personal commitments that included enjoying an evening dinner at a restaurant with friends. I believe that if she had known what was coming she wouldn't have left her post. But the relevant point for consideration is the likely impact she would have had if she had been at the command centre rather than keeping various other appointments. Would fewer people have died? Clearly, no. Could she have impacted the progress of the fire? Again, highly unlikely.

So if we accept that her presence would have had no meaningful impact on the outcome, why then was she so heavily criticised? Because she wasn't *present*, and that led people to believe that she didn't care and didn't understand the challenges the people faced, which I would reject on all accounts. Christine Nixon is a highly intelligent person. You do not become the first female Police Commissioner in Australia by chance. Her mistake on February 7 was not being present, and sadly her legacy was tainted by that.

If Nixon's legacy was bruised by her lack of presence, then some would argue that Prime Minister Scott Morrison's reputation was fatally undermined by his absence during 2019–20 bushfires that burned through NSW and Victoria. You would have to wonder who, if anyone, was advising him when he chose to fly to Fiji for a family beach holiday during what was the worst bushfire season experienced in decades.

The images of Morrison touring the south coast of NSW and trying to shake hands with exhausted Rural Fire Service volunteers was cringe-worthy. When he defended his absence by stating fatuously, 'I don't hold a hose', he convinced many that he was never going to win an election again. If ever a lack of presence conveyed a lack of compassion, empathy and understanding it was here. It was a direct failure of leadership and the Australian voting public punished him for it.

Compare the actions of Morrison with those of NSW Premier Gladys Berejiklian during the same bushfire crisis. It wasn't her role to hold a hose either, and from my knowledge that's not something she did. What she did do was turn up each day. She was with those in the control room leading the fight, she was in the affected communities and she was updating those of us who watched her morning briefings. This engagement demonstrated to us that she cared and she understood. We didn't expect her to be out there on the back of a fire truck, but we did expect her to be present. For a leader, those you are leading need to see you. Your presence conveys two messages: you care, and you understand the challenges they are facing. Your distance from those you are leading sends the converse message (whether accurate or not): that you are indifferent to and have no understanding of the challenges they are facing.

> *For a leader, those you are leading need to see you. Your presence conveys two messages: you care, and you understand the challenges they are facing.*

Too many leaders these days underestimate the significance of their presence with the teams they are leading, or the clients or customers they are trying to retain or win. Through a multitude of channels and devices we are today more 'connected' than at any time in history, yet in the most powerful way we are actually less connected. Observing and guiding events from a remote office, or from our lounge room during the evening with all the information we need in front of us, doesn't convey to those on the ground that we really care. The impression created is that we surely can't understand the challenges they are facing on the ground from our 'ivory tower'. Whether in fact we do or do not understand becomes irrelevant, because our absence creates the impression that we don't care.

Think of Sato Sun in that small fishing village in Japan. The community didn't expect him to have all the answers, they didn't expect him to be able to change things. What they got was his focused presence, and that was more than they could have expected.

WHAT I HAVE LEARNED

Clarity comes with action. True leaders don't have all the answers but they have the courage to make difficult decisions, and they understand the importance of being present, conveying to those they lead that they care and that they understand.

Certainly we need structure, policies and procedures. With these parameters we get consistency, but my experience in crisis situations is that we will often find a way to short-cut these formal structures for efficiency's sake. What is certain is that a balance is required between the formal process and policy we create and the innovation and creativity that often leads to the solution of complex problems. The leader's job is to navigate the field between policy and innovation.

WHAT CAN YOU DO?

Some of the greatest creators and innovators operate outside the rules and norms. Think of changes you could make that would sacrifice the predictability and safety of rules in order to encourage an environment of leading, innovation and creative decision making.

In leading through your own crisis or disaster, don't sit back or wait until you have all the answers to all the questions. You demonstrate leadership in the first instance simply by turning up and being present. Look for those opportunities to ask you team, 'How can I help?'

CHAPTER 5
LEAVE A LASTING IMPRESSION

When we meet someone for the first time we have the opportunity of leaving an indelible impression, and we can decide whether that is a good or a bad impression. Be it in a business or a social setting or greeting the waiter bringing us our evening meal, how we respond, what value we attach to the exchange will determine the impression we create. There is very little difference in energy needed between being memorable and being easily forgotten.

In the immediate aftermath of the tsunami and for the weeks that followed the bodies of the deceased victims were collected and transported to the temple at Wat Yan Yao, two hours' drive north of Phuket airport. Within a month a dedicated facility for the storage and forensic examination of the bodies was constructed at Tha Chat Chai, located halfway between the temple at Wat Yan Yao and the main police operations centre in Phuket. Surrounded by towering palm trees, the facility was constructed on some vacant land overlooking the Andaman Sea, just a couple of hundred metres away. It would have been an idyllic setting were it not for the 115 refrigerated shipping containers and their grim cargo.

For the first several months our hotel was located a couple of kilometres from the site, which meant a short drive home each afternoon. As the urgency of the response eased, and it became clear that the operation would last a good 12 months, it was incumbent upon those of us in leadership positions to manage the fatigue in our teams. This was felt on a physical level, but of greater concern to us was the emotional fatigue that was much harder to escape when dealing in death every day.

Be it in a business or a social setting or greeting the waiter bringing us our evening meal, how we respond, what value we attach to the exchange will determine the impression we create.

On our short drive home after a long day in the sun we would often call in at one of the local beachside bars to enjoy a short debrief over a cold Singha beer. It was surreal to sit at the water's edge, knowing that just weeks before that same water had swept in here at a height of several metres above our heads where we sat. Very clear evidence of the scale of destruction remained, but the spirit of the Thais could not be broken and they quickly returned to repair and reopen the local bars and restaurants. The problem was their customers had not returned.

We had started calling in for a beer and the occasional swim in the ocean as a way of cleansing ourselves from all we had done, touched and encountered during our shift. The salt of the ocean had great cleaning if not healing powers. What we came to realise pretty quickly was how much it meant to the local stall-holders for us to call in, and there was no doubt that our spend was all they were seeing most days. On later tours we had relocated our accommodation to the southern tip of the island of Phuket, an hour's drive from work.

Given the nature of our work, we didn't encourage unofficial visitors or members of the public. In the very early days families would come to the site imploring us to do more to find their loved ones, but we quite simply couldn't do more or give more than we were already. Foreign representatives of government and media would sometimes visit. So I wasn't surprised to be called by security one day and advised we had visitors who claimed to be relatives of a victim.

I stepped out of the air-conditioned demountable that served as my office and into the searing heat, a line of sweat immediately breaking out on my forehead. I walked to the security gate where I saw two people standing waiting for me who looked different from most of our visitors. They weren't dressed like government officials and didn't look like media. They clearly weren't Thai. The man looked to me to be in his thirties and was dressed casually in shorts and a t-shirt with a peaked cap; the woman was perhaps in her early twenties and dressed equally casually.

After introductions I learned they were German, which presented a problem. I spoke no German, and assumed they would speak little English. I was right in my assumption that they weren't government, media or from an embassy, wrong about their language skills. They had a look about them that was all too familiar to me, one that told me they were more important than any of the government, embassy or media visitors we were used to receiving.

I invited them to my office so we could escape the heat. By now we were all sweating copiously and anything seemed better than standing in the sun with a boom gate separating us.

We stepped into my office and the cool air had an immediate impact. By this stage the man had done all the talking and his companion had simply nodded with thanks when I handed her a bottle of cold water. They sat next to each other and I pulled up a chair to sit opposite them.

'How can I help?' I asked. I saw his chest rise as he drew in a deep breath. He looked up at the ceiling then turned to me with tears in his eyes. 'When you're ready,' I said, 'why don't tell me your story, or however much you feel comfortable sharing.' I slid a box of tissues towards them as he took her hand and held it tight.

They had a look about them that was all too familiar to me, one that told me they were more important than any of the government, embassy or media visitors we were used to receiving.

He began, 'I came to Thailand with my wife. It was our first holiday without the children.' There was a long pause as he composed himself before returning to the story. 'We were returning to this country for the first time since we were here for our honeymoon 25 years ago. The day before the tsunami was Christmas Day of course and we had been out to a restaurant that evening for a lovely dinner.

'Returning to the resort where we were staying, instead of heading straight up to our room we took a walk along the beach. The moon lit the sand and we walked along the water's edge holding hands, our feet in the water. It really was a beautiful evening and we felt lucky to share this time together.' By now the young woman was weeping silently. I had the feeling she was exhausted by grief.

He went on, 'We spoke about our life in Germany, how lucky we felt, and our plans for the future. We decided to go scuba diving in the morning, something we had done when we were first here.

'We usually took a walk before breakfast, but in the morning we had a late breakfast and then walked down to the water. As we walked along the beach we noticed the water had gone out much further than usual. It just seemed to keep going and exposing more sand. I have never seen anything like it. People were walking down towards the water's edge. And we just stood there staring out to sea.

'Then we saw it. A wall of water was coming towards us. I felt her grip my hand very tight. At first we didn't run. We couldn't move, we just stared. I think neither of us could make sense of what was happening. Then we turned to run, and even then I kept looking back and each time the wall of water was bigger and closer and was travelling so fast. We held onto each other and ran as fast as we could. The wave hit us and knocked us down. We hung onto each other while fighting to regain our feet. But there was no bottom. I opened my eyes while I was still under water and could see darkness and light. I moved towards the light and my head broke the surface. I pulled my wife up.

'She looked at me and I could see the fear in her eyes. The water continued to pound us and we were separated, the force of the water broke our grip and pulled me back under, and when I came to the surface again I couldn't see her. I screamed her name each time I came to the surface ... but I never saw her again.

'I thought I would die that day. Sometimes I wish I had.' He took a long, shuddering breath and again looked towards the ceiling, this time tears running freely down his cheeks. I saw a man who had grown used to shedding tears.

After a long silence he told me how he was finally pulled from the water. He lifted his shirt to show me the fresh scars that were healing faster than his heart. He told me how he had searched for his wife, refusing to believe she had died, hanging on to hope, as loved ones do, against all logic and common sense. He told me how he had gone to Wat Yan Yao to search among the bodies, until he had to return to Germany, to the family he'd left behind.

Four months later the local police visited him at his home to advise him that the body of his wife had been positively identified and would be returned to Germany, and that he should make arrangements for her funeral.

It was now August 2005. I asked him gently, 'Why have you come back now?'

He seemed to find strength in what he said next. 'I wanted to return to the hotel where we spent our last night together, to go to the restaurant where we had our last dinner together, and when I find the courage I want to go back to that place on the beach where I last saw her alive.'

I could understand his mission. Indeed, I thought it was an incredibly brave one such a short time after those terrible events.

I said, 'Fair enough, but why are you here today? How can I help you?'

He said, 'I want to understand the process you went through to identify my wife and what you can you tell me about her.'

So I explained the identification process we went through and how it gave us certainty when we finally confirmed the identification. I didn't have the specifics about his wife but told him that I would connect him with the German team here, who might have more information.

We were now well into the second hour and the young woman still hadn't said a word. I assumed she was unable to speak English. For the most part she sat with her head bowed. She too had that look of someone broken by pain. After we'd sat in silence for a while I turned to her. 'May I ask, why are you here?'

To my surprise she could speak good English. 'Like him. My mum was here on holiday. She died when the water hit. They found her and sent her home. We buried her.'

'Who was your mum on holiday with?'

She looked up at me, and for a split second a look of disbelief bordering on contempt passed across her face. 'Him!' was all she said.

Finally it dawned on me. 'He's your father!'

She looked at the man beside her, who was still holding her hand, and spoke in rapid German. I didn't need a translator to get the gist of what she was saying: 'This guy's an idiot. Hasn't he been listening?'

'My mum was here on holiday. She died when the water hit. They found her and sent her home. We buried her.'

Before they left we shared lunch in our makeshift canteen and I learned more about his wife and family. He shared photos of them, and for some strange reason I showed them photos of my kids. It was one more story from the shipping containers' sad tenants and those they left behind.

I called the German liaison officer and shared with her some of our exchange then arranged a car to convey them to the hotel occupied by the German team, and shortly after they left. As they drove off, with the two of them in the back seat, I saw her put her head on her father's shoulder and I'm sure both were weeping.

I felt privileged to have been allowed to spend that couple of hours in the very private world of this grieving family. I've said more than once that the most difficult part of my job in Thailand was dealing with the families of those lost, but the most rewarding part of my job in Thailand was dealing with the families of those lost.

I returned to my office, but now the air conditioning sent a chill through me.

I've said more than once the most difficult part of my job in Thailand was dealing with the families of those lost, but the most rewarding part of my job in Thailand was dealing with the families of those lost.

A few nights later I attended a gathering of the senior commanders of each of the countries represented. I don't recall the purpose of the event or the presentations made. What I do remember of that night is the German liaison officer approaching me.

'You know that German couple,' she asked, 'the man and his daughter that you spent time with and sent up to me?'

'Yes, of course,' I replied, already worrying that I might be the cause of a diplomatic rift by offending the daughter.

'They absolutely love you,' she said.

Much relieved, I was eager to hear the story.

She explained that the couple hadn't turned up at our site by chance. They had in fact already visited the German operation centre and had spoken with a member of the German team, who simply sent them down to me. She then told me of the deep impression I had made on them and the difference it had made. It had also given them many of the answers they were seeking.

Amongst so much death, misery and loss it felt good—no, it felt bloody fantastic—to hear that I had made a difference to that one grieving family.

I never saw them again, but I thought about them a lot, and it came to me that the German team member they had first met had forgotten what we were here for. He had forgotten our purpose.

We weren't there just to identify bodies. We were there to provide answers to grieving families. This man who had lost his wife didn't care about the other 5394 people—all he cared about was his wife. His daughter didn't care about the other bodies—all she cared about was her mother. Each time we interact with someone we have an opportunity to leave an indelible impression, and it is in our power to shape that impression.

Amongst so much death, misery and loss it felt good—no, it felt bloody fantastic—to hear that I had made a difference to that one grieving family.

When I reflect on what it was I gave them, it was nothing more than time. I encouraged him to tell his story, to be heard, to feel as though his experience was the only one that mattered, and for that couple of hours it was. It was so easy to be caught up in the enormity of our task. We had shipping containers filled with the bodies of loved ones. This man was just one of the thousands of relatives of those who filled our shipping containers. But for him at that point in time, his wife was the only one who mattered, because she was.

I didn't tell him much he didn't already know. I couldn't tell him how his wife was identified. I provided him with no more information about our process than he could have found with a Google search. We shared some time, a meal and I sent him back to the German operation centre where he had started his journey of discovery.

....

Each time we interact with someone we have an opportunity to leave an indelible impression, and it is in our power to shape that impression.

....

So why did our time together mean so much to them—and indeed to me, because I will always remember the two of them vividly and fondly? I remember how they were dressed. I remember how their handshakes lacked conviction and confidence. I remember the look of defeat they shared and the tears that ran freely down their cheeks. Yet it wasn't as though this was a one-off for me. For months on end this was all we did. Ultimately, I believe, when we give of ourselves without expectation of return, when we give our most valuable commodity, our time—that is what makes a lasting impression.

Whatever field we work in, be it finance, medicine, banking, building houses or driving buses, we build up a confidence or a level of tolerance for what at first might have been intimidating. Can you imagine driving a bendy bus through the CBD of Sydney or Melbourne and how incredibly intimidating that would be. I struggle with navigating my way through the dreaded hook turns in Melbourne to avoid being hit by a tram. When we first do it, whatever it is, it can be daunting and raise lots of big emotions.

When we give of ourselves without expectation of return, when we give our most valuable commodity, our time — that is what makes a lasting impression.

In 2009 I was diagnosed with a malignant melanoma and the first specialist I saw greeted me with, 'Who are you? Oh that's right, you're the aggressive tumour.' Not the sort of introduction to inspire confidence! The oncologist 'reassured' me, 'There are good survival rates from this', and I wanted to scream, 'When was anything other than survival an option!'

My point is, when we get comfortable with something we can lose perspective of its impact on others. Our everyday language can be haunting to someone hearing it for the first time. The German couple were dealing with the death of a wife and mother. It was the first and last time they would have to process this trauma. Ever. Yet we were dealing with countless bodies, working to identify someone's mum, someone's wife, every single day.

One of the most brilliant initiatives I observed in Bali when it came to dealing with the friends and families who remained after the bombings, determined not to leave the island without their loved ones, was around giving them permission to go. Of course, I don't mean this literally. They weren't officially granting them permission to leave the country by removing some hold over their passports. It was persuading the friends and relatives to give themselves permission to leave and accept by doing so they weren't abandoning their loved ones or mates.

By the time I arrived in Bali some days after the bombings, the task had shifted from care and repatriation of the injured to the recovery and identification of those who had died. The feelings

77

and emotions of those who had survived when their mates or family had not also shifted, which was completely understandable. For some, the shift in emotion was from shock, horror and grief to frustration, anger and denial. And sometimes we were blamed for standing in the way of releasing the bodies of their friends and family members. Again, totally understandable.

To address the rising frustration and anger over what the families and friends saw as unacceptable delays by us, something quite meaningful took place. Those with sufficient justification were invited to the hotel where the police were based and were given an insight into the processes that we were following to maintain the integrity of the identification process. The forensic procedures were explained, along with the possible implications of not getting it right by not following the correct steps. The families left that session better informed.

We didn't take away their anger or pain, but we did give them information, which increased their understanding. Having difficult conversations is best navigated by sharing the truth. When you give people information, you gain their understanding. Of course we knew the importance of the forensic procedures we were following, but that didn't mean everyone else did. Why would they? I couldn't drive a bendy bus through Sydney.

WHAT I HAVE LEARNED

When we are interacting with customers, clients and team members, what we say and how we say it matters. Our initial interaction will leave an indelible impression, and it is usually within our control to shape that impression. Often the time it takes to create a positive impression is no different from the time taken to leave a negative one. It's up to us how we decide to show up.

As leaders, we don't have to make everyone feel positive about the situation they find themselves in. You can't turn the loss of a wife or mother or daughter or son into a happy event. It may well be the worst day of their life, and you can't make it better. Hiding the truth, withholding information, is a judgement we are not necessarily entitled to make. When you share information you increase understanding, which allows for constructive, well-founded decision making.

WHAT CAN YOU DO?

There are a number of things you can do when engaging in really difficult conversations. First, recognise that it is not always your job to make everything right. Some situations can never be made right. Second, by deciding which facts to share and which to withhold you are potentially heading down a dangerous path. Later discovery of withheld facts compromises trust and can inflame past hurts. Third, ask yourself whether avoiding the hard conversation is about the other person's ability to cope or your own desire to avoid an uncomfortable situation.

PART II

THE
ACHIEVERS

The defining attributes of our achievers are not discretely set off from those of our leaders or our visionaries. They succeed not because of the absence of risk or the potential for failure, but through knowing that clarity and commitment serve us better than fear.

Achievers are seldom found celebrating their success or resting on their laurels, because they rarely see their job as done. There is always more to do, and that is where their focus is. Great achievers invest in the long game. They are rarely distracted by setbacks, losses or failures, because they are already changing tack and moving forward again. Their mission is clear, and they simply do not allow themselves to be distracted from the purposeful life they have chosen to live.

CHAPTER 6
MANAGE RISK, DON'T FEAR IT

It is always easier to remove or avoid risk than to manage it. There are competing interests, and those charged with reducing risk exposure and mitigating risk and potential harm will lean towards a strategy of avoidance. But the change makers, the innovators, the dreamers are less inclined to focus on the risk and reasons to say no in their pursuit of their goal. At the same time, as with most things, both extremes can be dangerous, unproductive and reckless.

I have never gone looking for projects that would increase our operations in Thailand. Our growth has always been on the back of circumstances where it appeared we could make a positive difference in a difficult situation. We have never been funded based on the number of kids we support or homes we build. We don't have it in our business plan to grow the number of kids or any measure that sees us increase in physical size. We celebrate the reuniting of families, of kids moving back to parents who were lost and are now found, or incapacitated but now capable. The ultimate reflection of sustained generational change would be that the need for our services no longer existed.

In 2010 I was working on a business project with a Thai woman living in Australia and at the end of one of our sessions she was talking to me about a charity founder in Thailand. I had never heard of the charity or the founder. She came from a town whose name I couldn't even pronounce or readily find on a map. 'She cares for children with HIV, and many of them have died. They continue to die because she can't provide the medicine they need.' I didn't know it then but that casual conversation would change lives, none more than mine.

Janet told me more about this woman and her work, and the more questions I asked the more I felt drawn in. 'Why don't we give her a call?' We sat at my office desk and Janet called her and spoke in Thai, translating each of my questions. 'I need to go and meet her,' I said. I flew to Bangkok, took an internal flight to a place called Ubon Ratchathani and then drove myself to the town of Yasothon. Off a side road on the edge of town was a home for children, delightfully called Baan Home Hug. Here I met Khru Prateep and Khun Rotjana. Stepping into this place, and knowing at least two friendly faces, I finally began to relax.

It felt as though the better days were behind this home and life now was a daily struggle of a kind I could scarcely comprehend.

My immediate impression of Baan Home Hug was of a place that was doing it tough. The buildings looked very tired and in need of repair, the kitchen was as basic as it comes, consisting of three free-standing gas burners. All the kids had a similar look about them: they were skinny, like they were short of a good feed and were just hanging on. Like their surroundings they needed some maintenance.

It felt as though the better days were behind this home and life now was a daily struggle of a kind I could scarcely comprehend. What especially brought this home to me, when I visited the room where the kids slept with Khru Prateep and the woman who ran the show, was the beds the kids slept in. They were broken-down hospital beds that had been discarded by the local hospital. Everything about the place just felt sad and wrong. The only exception was the love that clearly existed between the kids and the woman in charge. Without knowing the kids, their story, the history or the people who ran it, I just felt like these kids deserved more.

My first meeting with this strange person wasn't what you would call love at first sight. After the guided tour of the home we sat down to talk and learn about each other. Given that I didn't speak Thai and she didn't speak English, we were guided through the conversation by Khru Prateep, who spoke both fluently.

Her name was Mae Thiew. In the Thai way, that is not her formal name but the name that she is best known by. Mae Thiew was dressed in extra-large, baggy clothes and more layers than seemed suitable in this climate. Though she was in her mid forties, she had her hair gathered in two pigtails.

The conversation started politely enough, but it soon took a turn as Khru Prateep and Mae Thiew both spoke in Thai. I would come to learn that Mae Thiew is not one to hide her emotion. She speaks her mind and her truth, and is not afraid of upsetting anyone. To some degree she is most un-Thai for these reasons.

As we sat in a triangle I was of course unable to follow their conversation but I was getting a feeling that I wasn't particularly welcome. I have found that it usually takes a few meetings before people decide that they don't like me, but she had arrived at that point at rocket speed!

As the conversation became more animated Mae Thiew looked at me with what seemed almost like hatred. More than a decade on, that look in her eyes has never left me. Thankfully it was the only time I have ever had that look from her, but it stung. Khru Prateep caught the look and realised I understood enough of what was happening here to be somewhat alarmed.

Khru Prateep then said to me, 'I haven't told her what you do. I will do that now.' Then she spoke in a calming manner and I can only assume with calming words, as she does. Because a transformation came over Mae Thiew and I saw a softness fill her eyes and a smile that I would come to know so well.

Mae Thiew's journey started in Bangkok where she grew up and went to university. Her degree required that she complete a placement in the field before she graduated. She chose to head to Chiang Rai in the far north of Thailand and to work among the hill tribes that occupied that region.

There she would be confronted by an ugliness that many Thais associate only with foreign men—the sex trade. It was within these remoter regions far from the seedy bars, massage parlours and bright lights that the trafficking of children into the sex industry was occurring. Mae Thiew came across young boys and girls who were trafficked by those they should have been able to trust most, their parents. But their parents were often not much more than children themselves and were only doing what had been done to them. Frequently trafficked to pay a debt, they were merely repeating what they had inherited.

Young girls working in the sex trade were giving birth to children who were born with HIV. These young mothers often couldn't care for themselves, let alone a newborn, and faced an emotional, physical and financial burden they were ill-equipped to manage. The children were unwanted because of the impossible hardship their arrival brought.

Mae Thiew had found her purpose and calling. She returned to Bangkok, sold all her possessions and left the city with a pocketful of cash and a commitment to help these children. Between the hill tribes of Chiang Rai and Bangkok was Yasothon, a place that would become home for her and the children that no one seemed to want. I imagine she didn't expect the ensuing years to be easy, but I wonder if she could have anticipated the struggles she would face.

Baan Home Hug was now well past its glory days, its peeling paint like the scales rising off a dead fish. The cracked and broken windows gave it a hard look; at first glance you could be forgiven for thinking it had been abandoned years ago. It had not always been like this, of course, and I know from experience the pride that Mae Thiew would have felt as the first bricks were laid, the building took shape and the doors were hung. And she would have been right in the middle of it all, snatching the trowel out of the brickie's hand if he was too slow or not doing it right—that's her, she can't help herself!

I imagine she didn't expect the ensuing years to be easy, but I wonder if she could have anticipated the struggles that she would face.

In those early days there were funders and backers, believers and supporters—their names are on the side of the buildings they contributed to. They too are faded and tired looking now. I suspect many years have passed since they last visited.

Yasothon is the smallest province in the lower northeast of Thailand's Isan region and is a seven-hour drive from Bangkok, or an hour's flight to Ubon Ratchathani followed by an hour-long drive. The region of Ubon and Yasothon is farming country and pretty much devoid of tourists. The town of Yasothon sits on the Chi River, but even that is not sufficient to draw tourists unless they are fascinated by toads. The town very proudly hosts a toad museum and the largest toad statue in Thailand, though I doubt there's much competition when it comes to toad statues.

The museum is built inside a 19-metre, five-story-high toad. You enter the museum through its belly, I kid you not. Surely, though, the highlight of your visit is ascending the internal stairs to the viewing platform located in, where else, the toad's mouth. It gives sweeping views of a rather boring vista, to be honest. But it's not the giant toad that brings me to town.

Setting up home in Yasothon, where land was affordable, meant having enough space to let the kids run free. It also gave her the privacy she sought for the kids, but at what price? I have long since discovered that it's hard for people to support and connect with a cause when they can't 'see' it.

There is a balance to be struck. I completely understand the challenge she faced. It's one we at *Hands* continue to juggle almost 20 years on. Donors and sponsors connect and give when they understand and are moved by the cause. They are more likely to make a personal and financial commitment when their head and heart are engaged. Without that connection, the fundraising becomes harder the greater the separation between them and the cause.

> *I have long since discovered that it's hard for people to support and connect with a cause when they can't 'see' it.*

How much of the story of the kids is appropriate to share? How about none? How about allowing the kids to live in complete privacy, letting them decide when they are old enough to tell their own story as and if they choose. But what if the funds needed to sustain their lives aren't raised and the kids don't live to an age when they can decide whether or not to share their story? At Baan Home Hug the kids were dying with their story intact, their privacy protected. Cremating the bodies of eight-year-olds who die from treatable illness surely can't be an acceptable price for protecting their privacy.

I see a growing trend to implement policy, rules and legislation that seem to start from a place that everyone is a potential felon looking to harm, abuse or objectify children. Certainly we need to protect those in society who are incapable of protecting themselves, but we also need to consider the implications of our actions when we seek to remove all risk. The increasing reach of well-meaning but sometimes damaging policy is not just confined to this area. In seeking to control a small but pernicious minority, we are quick to impose rules and legislation on the majority that can have long-term unintended consequences. As society becomes more litigious, we move to mitigate the exposure of shareholders and decision makers where it's simply easier to remove risk. We design policy and legislation around those with ill intent, rather than serving the vast majority who are inherently well-meaning.

Cremating the bodies of eight-year-olds who die from treatable illnesses surely can't be an acceptable price for protecting their privacy.

At Baan Home Hug we have two decades of evidence of what happens when there is next to zero visibility between donors and the kids. Because of insufficient funds to purchase medicines, children died. When their story became known, when we built connection, we were able to generate income and purchase the medicine, and as a result something remarkable happened, the children stopped dying.

The charity sector has become incredibly competitive, with so many organisations, all doing great work, competing for the limited spend of donors, whether individuals or businesses. As a result, if you can't present a story that appeals to the head and heart of a donor, then it is near-on impossible to generate the emotion that leads to action. People won't support what they can't see. Visibility gives them reasons to believe and to trust.

Baan Home Hug offers a simple but pretty compelling object lesson of this. Without knowledge of their needs, the children died; with knowledge and connection, they lived.

For Mae Thiew, raising money in the early years was the easy part. She had a compelling story and inexhaustible energy to travel advocating on behalf of the children and the work she was doing. Funding came from those who could see a building erected with their name on it, a monument to their good will. But people moved on and found some other cause to support, and then it got harder. In my experience working with many start-up charities in Australia, this is universally true. The initial success rides on the gravitas of the founder, how deep their pockets are and how much stamina they have. Mae Thiew's journey was no different.

I didn't find out about the problem of insufficient funds for essential medicines on my first visit. It would take many trips over that first year to learn of this and so much more. But I saw enough on that first trip to know that we could help here. I knew we had the capacity, and for me that meant we had to do something. I couldn't unsee what I had seen and I couldn't pretend that these kids mattered any less than the kids who had survived the tsunami.

Driving back to Ubon for my return flight after that first trip I thought about Mae Thiew's reaction to me during the meeting. It was a clear sign that she protected those children fiercely and didn't trust outsiders, which in my view was a good thing. Here I was, a white middle-aged male, walking into her home for kids, many of whom had known sexual abuse before she found them, and suggesting I might be able to help. The charity sector welcomes many well-meaning people who offer help, who say they want to get involved, who say they will return, but who never do. Why would Mae Thiew think I was any different from the rest who had promised much and delivered little.

I made several trips to Yasothon in 2010, and each time I visited we built a little more trust. I'm sure she was surprised each time I returned, and I could tell by the reaction of the kids that they weren't used to visitors, certainly not foreign visitors, who keep coming back.

The charity sector welcomes many well-meaning people who offer help, who say they want to get involved, who say they will return, but who never do.

Parking my humanitarian urge and taking an evidence-based approach to the problem, I knew we had the capacity to do something meaningful for Mae Thiew and the children of Baan Home Hug. I presented to the board at *Hands* a simple but I thought compelling case: 'I believe we can stop children dying if we provide them with support.' It couldn't have been simpler. I evidently presented it persuasively enough because I soon returned to Baan Home Hug with the endorsement of the *Hands* board.

Taking on the responsibility of supporting Baan Home Hug was another example of our approach of not getting too caught up in the enormity of the challenge and not needing to have all of the answers to all of the questions before we started. It was a case of committing to do what we could within our means and working together to find the solutions to the bigger challenges.

We can always find reasons not to do something, arguments for why it is outside our remit or a departure from our origins. We point out that we have no connection to the region and cite the lack of history between the parties. But when we decide to focus on the results and not the excuses, we are capable of achieving so much more, and if we do nothing then nothing will change.

Were there risks in supporting a partner about whom, in all honesty, we knew very little? Of course there were. It would be a huge departure for us, and in truth there was a mixed response from a number of key supporters when the idea of taking on Baan Home Hug was presented to them. But the way the board saw it was that there was a far greater risk to the children in doing nothing. Of course *Hands* could distance ourselves from risk associated with a new venture, but we believed the difference we could bring to the lives of the kids and that community far outweighed any risk. When risk is viewed in isolation from potential reward we will always err on the side of caution, because that is the job of those charged with risk mitigation—to remove and reduce exposure.

We started by offering financial support for the renovation of the site—updating the water collection and storage facilities, building new kitchens, refurbishing the rooms the kids slept in and replacing those depressing hospital beds. But the biggest burden we removed from Mae Thiew was the awful challenge of deciding who would receive the life-giving medicine and who would not. We provided for access to the medicines and the health services that all of the kids needed and deserved.

The more time I spent with Mae Thiew, the more projects we brought to her home, until our continuing engagement finally convinced her that the community of *Hands* was different. When we left and said we would be back, we returned. We did what we said we would do and so built trust.

The biggest burden we removed from Mae Thiew was the awful challenge of deciding who would receive the life-giving medicine and who would not.

As Mae Thiew came to learn more about what we did at *Hands*, she learned of these bike rides that we used to raise funds for the homes, including her own. After the first year in 2009, we ensured that we included either kids or staff from one of our homes on the rides so they got to experience the ride through Thailand. For many of the Thais who rode with us we were taking them to parts of their country they had never seen and exposing them to experiences they didn't know existed. It wasn't long after Mae Thiew and I arrived at a point where we both accepted that our relationship would be an enduring one that she told me she wanted to ride with us. I was delighted, but also surprised. I asked her why and her response has never left me.

She explained that each day she would gather the children after school and talk to them about life lessons and a key theme was always gratitude. The kids should be grateful for what they have and for those who support them, was how Mae Thiew explained it to me. Initially I thought that was a valid lesson to be teaching anyone, but then I reflected on who the audience was.

These were kids whose individual stories I choose not to share out of respect for their privacy but also because many people simply wouldn't believe me. These kids for whom life had been such an unbelievably cruel struggle were being lectured on the social graces around gratitude.

What is it about those who have the least in terms of what we might measure as wealth, happiness and success that makes them seem to understand gratitude the best? In my experience, the greater their struggle and the less they have, the more they appreciate what they are given. When we fight hard for something, we come to appreciate and attach more value to it than if there is no fight, sacrifice or struggle.

I have spent many hours over the past two decades watching these kids share. They share their food, their clothes, their shoes. They share the moment. It might be a moment of joyful play, it might be cultural dance or a sad memory, but they share.

I often wonder whether in western societies there is a correlation between the ease with which our basic needs are met, the lack of struggle we experience, and the rise in mental health issues. Do we build resilience, both mental and physical, from the struggles we avoid? When we remove risk from our lives, when we define the boundaries, when we establish a pathway rather than encouraging the explorers and adventurers, are we in fact doing a disservice to those we seek to protect the most?

If all our needs are met, the boundaries are set and the rules are clear, what muscle memory have we built to sustain us when the boundaries are absent? Each day I spent with them I was learning from these kids about what gratitude was, what resilience was truly about and why I had so much more to learn.

Do we build resilience, both mental and physical, from the struggles we avoid?

Mae Thiew's decision to ride with us reminded me of how I make a lot of decisions. It seemed like the right thing to do; 'yes' was the answer even without fully understanding the experience or the commitment required. The fact that she didn't ride a bike, didn't own a bike and thought that all she needed was a couple of training rides on a borrowed bike in the two weeks leading up to the 800 km ride didn't set her up well.

The last day on the bike, on any tour, is special. Your energy is up, as is your excitement for tackling the final stretch heading home. Riding with Mae Thiew, watching how she sets aside the physical challenges, is always a special experience, but the final day is always different again. For her that final day finishes at her home, while we are just visitors she invites in for a couple of hours. At breakfast you will see her with newfound energy and excitement as she musters the riders in her eagerness to get on the road. The sooner we're on the bikes, the sooner we'll reach Baan Home Hug and the children.

As the riders gathered around their bikes on that final morning, applying sunscreen, filling water bottles and going through their morning routines, Mae Thiew came over to me. Before embracing the life of a monk, whose many rules include a prohibition from touching a male, she used to give me the strongest of hugs. The strength and the genuine exchange of love that occurred during those hugs is something I miss. But this particular morning we enjoyed a long hug and when she released me she took me by my shoulders and looked deep into my eyes. Her eyes were filled with tears and in her best English she said to me, 'For 26 years I have not trusted a man. Now I trust you. I can die happy now. Thank you, Khun Peter.'

If the ride is the fundraising reward, then the finish brings it all together and is food for the soul. From the time they climb onto their bike the riders are riding towards the home they have been supporting to meet the kids they have spent 9 to 12 months talking about and working for. The end of the ride. I can't explain it. To truly understand, it has to be experienced. It is the slowest part of the journey. The closer we get to home, the slower the riders pedal, as if they don't want it to end and are seeking to put off their arrival as long as they can.

As we weave our way home, the pace slows, the chat between the riders is like that of kids on Christmas Eve, and many will shed more than a few tears as they reflect on their achievement. The first sign that we are really close is the noise—the drums and musical instruments, the cheers and screams of the kids when they know we are close. By this time I have normally found my way to the back of the riding group so I can watch everyone, particularly the first-timers, savour their own experience. You only get this feeling once. After leading more than 30 rides in Thailand, I love to watch the riders go through this for the first time. It is pandemonium as kids dart in between the bikes, and riders laugh and cry. It is a unique moment of pure unbridled joy that is unequalled in my experience.

Over the next couple of hours we enjoy lunch between more hugs and tears and stories and reflections. Again, I love to watch the riders and their differing responses. Some will jump up and dance with the kids; others will turn inwards and sit in deep reflection and pass no more than a head nod in unspoken recognition of what has just occurred. The end of the ride doesn't just bring the experience together; it binds the riders around an experience they won't forget. Ever.

They will go home and talk about the ride, about the companionship, the struggles and celebrations, and they will talk about the kids. And it might just happen that someone they talk to says, 'I think I'd like to do that ride,' and then we have another rider who will fundraise and provide the means to keep the kids fed and healthy and in school and, most importantly, alive. Surely any risk-averse alternative to 'protect' the kids is no alternative at all. For me, it is very clear that if we take away the connection by isolating the riders from the homes, we revert to status quo before *Hands'* involvement.

It is pandemonium as kids dart in between the bikes, and riders laugh and cry. It is a unique moment of pure unbridled joy that is unequalled in my experience.

Some people, no doubt with good intent, have criticised us for inviting our riders to visit the kids at the end of their 800 km journey. Many of the riders have made a commitment of up to a year from the time they signed up to the last day on the bike. They need to pay for their own tour costs and to train for the ride of between 500 km and 1600 km. As one of our past riders, Steve Ford, has said, 'I fundraise for the kids, but I ride for myself.'

The fundraising is a non-negotiable element of the ride; it is a powerful journey that connects the rider to the cause, forcing them to commit not just to *Hands* but to the journey and their own learning.

Looking to engage a new tour provider to lead our tours through Thailand I was connected to an organisation that operated across a number of different countries. I liked their operations and enjoyed the level of service they offered. I looked to deepen the relationship in the years after COVID to set us up for the years to follow. I would be bringing them significant business based on the number of rides we led each year. We shared an appetite to work together, but due to their size of operations and the commercial aspect of the business I learned that our model would need to be approved by a number of internal risk committees. The end result: we were told that to work together our rides would need to finish somewhere other than our homes.

What they were proposing was that we assemble a group of people who would spend the best part of a year fundraising to support the kids in our homes. Then they would ride to the home, but pull up short and not actually visit the home or the kids. The rationale was the potential risk posed by our riders to the kids.

I suggested two compelling counter-arguments. First, since 2009 *Hands* had facilitated some 40 rides that finished at one or another of our homes. Over that entire time there hadn't been a single incident of any rider behaviour having a negative impact on the kids. I suggested that pulling up short and not visiting the homes not only took away a massive part of why we rode in Thailand, but also undermined trust between us and the riders. Effectively we were asking them to fundraise and ride for us, but we didn't trust them enough to see or visit the kids' homes. How could we with integrity ask the riders to fundraise on our behalf but then not allow them to see where their funds went? An absurd suggestion any way you look at it.

The second argument I presented was devoid of emotion and simply based on objective evidence. I outlined the history of the children dying for lack of support when no one visited them and no connections were made. I then presented evidence of the change that was achieved once we introduced the kids to our community. Simply put, the kids stopped dying. When people had visibility and connection they cared and they raised money.

The position of the company remained unchanged. They were set on removing as much risk exposure as possible even though the bigger implication of what they were imposing would in time lead to the return to the death of children. For me this is what happens when people maintain a single-minded focus on risk. Their job is to find potential exposure points and remove them. The bigger picture is not their concern. Perhaps the view of those in risk mitigation would be more balanced and they might see things differently if half their week was spent on driving revenue and growth to the business.

In our efforts to get things right, to find the right balance, we can't let perfect be the enemy of good. If we're waiting for perfection, well, we might just never get started.

Without connection and engagement, effective fundraising won't happen and the kids won't get the medicine they need. We can always find reasons and excuses for inaction and 'what ifs'. We can write policy and procedure with the best of intentions, but just because we find evidence to justify our bias doesn't mean that it should apply in all cases and for everyone.

In our efforts to get things right, to find the right balance, we can't let perfect be the enemy of good. If we're waiting for perfection, well, we might just never get started. We need courageous leaders who acknowledge and manage risk rather than ones who are defined and guided by fear.

WHAT I HAVE LEARNED

I have come to learn that when raising kids, building a business or running a charity, it is easier to eliminate risk than to have the courage and strength to manage it. We learn to manage risk by facing it, not by erasing it. In difficult times we learn to make difficult and complex decisions. If we live our lives and raise our kids according to rigidly defined guidelines, avoiding or removing risk at every opportunity and attempting to predict outcomes, we shouldn't be surprised to see a generation incapable of making difficult decisions. Our greatest innovators and artists work outside of defined parameters and rules, thereby creating and discovering new solutions.

Operating without due consideration to risk is negligent and can potentially expose business owners and directors to prosecution when they don't have risk mitigation strategies in place, but avoiding risk is not the answer either.

In my former life in the police there was inherent risk every time someone turned up for a shift. For those involved in the execution of high-risk search warrants or arrests, there was always the possibility of injury or worse for those first through the door. Not making the arrest or executing the warrant because of the potential risk was not an option. Planning and risk assessments were conducted, but the job got done. Since it couldn't be avoided, it had to be managed.

WHAT CAN YOU DO?

If you are in a position of influence in your place of work, is there the opportunity to challenge self-imposed (rather than government-mandated) policy and procedure?

As a leader, do you have the courage to make decisions and seize opportunities rather than erring on the side of caution?

Our kids will build muscle memory from facing different challenges. How do we expect them to manage risk and make informed judgement calls as adults if we seek to remove all the risk during their formative years? Risk analysis and critical decision making are learned skills that need to be practised. We need to manage risk rather than avoiding it at every opportunity.

CHAPTER 7
MODEL A LIFE WELL LIVED

While life is finite we seldom know when it will be exhausted. We like to believe it is endless or at least ignore how tenuous our hold on it is. Our time, how we share it and what difference we seek to make is the yardstick by which we are measured. 'The purpose of life,' wrote the philosopher poet Ralph Waldo Emerson, 'is not to be happy. It is to be useful, to be honorable, to be compassionate, to have it make some difference that you have lived and lived well.'

Growing up in the slums of Khlong Toei in Bangkok was always going to leave a lasting impression on Khun Rotjana's character and mindset. But from my experience that impression will not necessarily be the obvious one. Living in an environment where everything is a struggle can either generate resentment and anger or build resolve and gratitude. It can foster a will to escape the poverty and build a life beyond the struggle or trigger a fight against those who fail to understand the challenges they face.

Khun Rotjana grew up in the slums and decided that education was her way forward. While she didn't necessarily see it as a way out, it was certainly a pathway towards a brighter future for her and her family. Supported by Khru Prateep and the Duang Prateep Foundation, Khun Rotjana would be one of the first graduates from a school set up in the slums to give children a chance to avoid the life of poverty and struggle they were destined to lead.

Living in an environment where everything is a struggle can either generate resentment and anger or build resolve and gratitude.

The school was established by Khru Prateep who has spent her entire life fighting for those society likes to pretend don't exist. She gave a voice to those who are not heard or are ignored by change makers. Khru Prateep believed that the best chance the children of the slums had was through education, but for many attending the local school wasn't an option so she created her own school. Initially it was shut down by the government. She reopened it and they shut it down. Again she reopened it and this time the government decided it would be easier to work with her than against her. Khru Prateep would eventually be awarded as 'teacher of the year' by those who had repeatedly tried to shut her down.

Khun Rotjana was an early graduate of the school and would continue her studies to become an educator herself. She was living and working in Khong Toei when the tsunami struck in 2004 more than a thousand kilometres away. It would change her life forever. In the days and weeks that followed the true toll of that devastating event was becoming clear.

For every life lost there were families who would never be whole again. Thirty-two children, having lost their families, were taken to a temple at Bang Muang, 14 km south of Wat Yan Yao, where an international team of highly trained specialists were at work identifying tsunami victims, undoubtedly including these children's own parents. A tent was erected at the temple to provide shelter for the children. It's not lost on me that though I went to Thailand tasked with identifying the bodies of the victims, it was the surviving children of those victims who would have the greatest and most enduring impact on my life, as for Khun Rotjana.

As the number of kids at the temple grew, Khun Rotjana was asked if she would leave Bangkok with her daughter Ton Palm to provide care for them. Answering the call, Khun Rotjana headed south and took up residence in the tent with the kids. Eventually a home was built for her and the children she cared for at Baan Tharn Namchai.

Arriving for the opening of the home in 2006, I initially believed my job was done, that *Hands Across the Water*, which had been formed some 12 months before, had served its purpose and I could return to Australia to my life as a dad of three kids and my forensic duties with the NSW Police. I could retire my role as a charity worker, which to be honest I knew bugger all about and had just fumbled my way through. Surely building the home was all the kids needed, right?

As the car pulled away from Baan Tharn Namchai that day with the pomp and ceremony over, I looked out of the car window and I thought, *What happens to these kids now? Who supports them?* It came to me clearly that the job of *Hands* was far from done. In fact, it had only just started, as had my relationship with Khun Rotjana.

The fundraising I had done to contribute to the build of the first home was less than traditional. My commitment to fundraise to build the home didn't bring with it any wisdom, or practical plans, or throngs of philanthropists coming forward to support the cause. I had been invited by Matt Church, a well-known corporate speaker on the Australian circuit, to share my story with audiences. I dismissed out of hand the idea that I had anything of value to share. I was just a police officer. What could I possibly offer those in corporate or anyone else outside of policing or counterterrorism. It was only after I met the kids for the first time that I reflected on Matt's suggestion and decided that even if half of what he had to say was true, it could be a great way to raise funds through the speaking fees.

In the days following the opening of Baan Tharn Namchai I spent a lot of time thinking about the home, the kids and Khun Rotjana's role moving forward. I had never really thought about how this ended, let alone who would pick up the fundraising tab when I returned to Australia. In a hugely naive way I had assumed the best thing we could do was build a real home for the kids living in a tent, but I hadn't thought through what came next. Building a home might very well address immediate needs, but it brought with it a lifetime of costs to keep the building operational.

Returning to Australia, I became fully aware of the responsibility that came with building the home. Now we had to meet the costs of keeping the kids fed, the staff employed and the building maintained to a suitable standard. I recognised that I couldn't count on someone stepping forward and offering to meet the recurrent costs. If anything, the opposite was happening. As time passed, offers of support were dwindling. We had to find a different way to engage potential donors.

At the same time, I was finding that the keynote speaking I was doing in front of an ever-widening range of audiences was working. With each presentation I had the opportunity to share the story of the work I was doing and the work still to be done. I was getting paid regularly and sometimes clients and audiences were making donations, but the clearest affirmation that this model was working came in San Francisco in 2007.

I was invited to speak at the NARTA conference, which was a gathering of the senior executives of members and suppliers in the electrical retail industry. I delivered a keynote presentation on the last day of the conference, and what followed changed many lives and would set *Hands Across the Water* in a direction that would have been unlikely to occur otherwise. A member of the audience asked about the recurrent costs of running Baan Tharn Namchai. I replied that they were A$50000 per annum. (They are now closer to A$2 million.) Then one of the delegates threw out a challenge to match the $500 donation he was making. Within hours the total had reached $100000 and by dinner it had hit $250000. I would leave that conference with a commitment of $250000 towards the work that I had started in Thailand. I hadn't asked for donations. I didn't lay out a shopping list of our needs. I just shared a few stories that resonated with the audience.

In the years that followed this spontaneous act of generosity would be repeated on half a dozen occasions when a donation of $250000 or more would be made. Again, there was no ask, no ultimatum presented to the audience that if I didn't raise a certain amount of money by the end of the day, tragedy would befall the children we support. I just told a few stories.

I believe the vast majority of people and businesses want to lift others up. They want to contribute, to make a difference, to see those who have been dealt a bad hand get a fair go. Sometimes they just need to be offered a pathway that leads them towards that giving and that ability to genuinely bring hope to someone's life.

After the conference, while sitting in the airport lounge waiting for my return flight to Australia, I received an email from Khun Rotjana advising me that she had been diagnosed with advanced and aggressive breast cancer. Given the shortcomings of the public health system in Thailand, there was no certainty that she would survive the wait time.

That conference in San Francisco not only became a source of immediate and (as it would prove) ongoing funding for *Hands*, but it delivered into my life a number of incredibly giving and inspiring people. Kay Spencer was the CEO of NARTA at the time and we immediately formed a partnership that has endured and grown stronger over the decade and a half since. Kay later joined our board and not long after took on the role of Chair to guide us towards opportunity and a greater purpose. Together, Kay and I, along with the *Hands* board, committed to supporting Khun Rotjana and ensuring she had access to the private health care system to give her the best chance of fighting the cancer that had invaded her body.

I always loved seeing the adoring looks the kids had for her and how, with a few words and a beaming smile, she would ensure that each of those hundred-plus kids went to bed feeling special and loved, because they were.

Khun Rotjana underwent surgery, which left her physically and emotionally scarred, but it also gave her back her health and if anything strengthened her resolve to fight for the children in her care. In the years that followed I would spend more time with Khun Rotjana as my trips to Thailand increased in frequency. Several highlights in my time with her come to mind.

After dinner we would sit in the still of the night as the kids started to head for bed, and they would come down freshly showered with talcum powder on their faces to say goodnight. I always loved seeing the adoring looks the kids had for her and how, with a few words and a beaming smile, she would ensure that each of those hundred-plus kids went to bed feeling special and loved, because they were.

I could always count on an emotional experience when finishing one of our rides at BTN and being welcomed by Khun Rotjana. For our January rides this was the end of a 1600 km journey that took a couple of weeks. I would arrive physically spent and the last day was always an emotional one.

The final day on the southern ride from Bangkok to Khao Lak finishes with a reflection session at the temple, which had been the final destination for all those lost family members of the staff and kids at BTN. As the years passed and the number of kids at BTN who had lost relatives in the tsunami fell, the temple never lost its power over me. I would share with the riders the purpose of the temple, the work we did after its transformation from a place of worship, peace and solitude to one of death and tragedy, and its eventual return to a spiritual home once again.

The final kilometres from the temple at Wat Yan Yao to our destination at Baan Tharn Namchai end with a right-hand turn off the main road and for the last two hundred metres we are drawn on by the sounds of the drums and children's voices that signal our homecoming. I would always feel the welcome from Khun Rotjana, who never minded a sweaty hug. For me her embrace was always something special. She herself never rode, but I felt she understood the journey we were on and what we had left out on the road.

In 2017 Khun Rotjana's health started to fail her. After a persistent bout of illness she was admitted to hospital in Surat Thani. When you have been on a journey with a cancer survivor and you hear that they are unwell it takes on a heightened significance. After a concerned call from Game, a former student of Baan Tharn Namchai's now working for *Hands* as our General Manager based in Bangkok, I booked a flight to Thailand for the next day.

I flew in to Bangkok then took a connecting flight down to Surat Thani, where I was met by some of the staff from Baan Tharn Namchai. We drove to the hospital with little conversation, but I was jolted as we turned into the Surat Thani Cancer Centre. The 'Thai Wellness Centre' might have offered a more comforting welcome. It was one of those times in life when you're hoping the feeling you have in your gut is wrong. But it wasn't.

She herself never rode, but I felt she understood the journey we were on and what we had left out on the road.

Walking into Khun Rotjana's private room I saw a frightened girl lying in the bed. For a moment I felt like her father and she had been waiting for me to arrive. Her hug had none of the strength and confidence I knew so well. It was weak and lacked the conviction that would tell me everything would be all right. As we hugged I felt the tears running down her face, and I knew this was different.

The staff from BTN who were in the room soon left and I was alone with Khun Rotjana. She pointed to an envelope on the bedside table. I picked it up and to my surprise the letter was addressed to me. I opened it, assuming it was something to do with BTN and they had merely used the hospital stationary. But it was handwritten in English and on hospital letterhead. I glanced down to the bottom and saw it was signed off by a hospital doctor. I scanned the letter with dread and was chilled by the words that jumped off the page: 'bone metastasis', 'cancer returned' and, most jarring, 'palliative care'.

I read back over the letter and before I could finish it a second time Khun Rotjana looked up at me with a fear in her eyes that I had never seen before and said, 'What is wrong with me? Is the cancer back?'

I felt my stomach turn. I was jolted to realise that no one from the medical staff or her own staff had told her what was wrong and that for some reason the doctor had thought I should know before her. Evidently they were looking for me to break the news and explain the contents of the letter. I had of course much experience in delivering the most harrowing of news to families, but I'd had time to prepare for that, and it was my job.

I felt exposed and compromised, and my heart was breaking for this amazing woman lying here without answers and hoping I would deliver good news. But I had nothing to offer but bad news. I hadn't had a chance to develop the script or choose my words. I felt a chill run through my body as Khun Rotjana put her hand on my arm and asked again, 'Will I be okay?'

I read the letter again, desperately hoping the words had changed, but the message was clear and the prognosis, as I understood it, was as bad as it gets. I took her hand in mine and explained that she was very sick, that the cancer had returned and it had spread through her body. Incorrectly, I understood 'palliative' to mean the care of a terminal patient with little time, rather than the care of someone with little hope of cure.

I sought out one of the treating doctors. I wanted to say first, 'What was everyone thinking in giving me that letter without any notice or warning?' But I could only assume it was in some way out of respect for the position I held and my role in her life that the doctor decided to write to me. Together we spoke to Khun Rotjana and delivered to her the news that no one ever wants to hear, or to deliver.

My time at the hospital was brief. I had arrived in Thailand from Sydney the evening before and would be leaving later that afternoon.

The first thing I tried to do was ignore the words on the page and deny the severity. The second was to believe there was a way this could be turned around. Surely she could beat this — she'd done it before and could do it again. This was Khun Rotjana, after all.

The trip back to Bangkok and then on to Sydney was a lonely one and I spent a lot of time in my head trying to convince myself it would be okay, but deep down I knew the odds were against her. The word *palliative* kept rising off the page, telling me that this had just got very real and serious. I thought about Khun Rotjana and how broken she was. I thought about her daughter, Ton Palm, and the irony that she had spent the past 10 years living in a home with her mum surrounded by kids who had lost their parents, and she was now faced with the very real prospect of losing her own mum. I thought about how cruel life could be and wondered how, on any level, Khun Rotjana's life of service to others could be so rewarded. Sometimes life is just unfair, and karma didn't seem to be playing out here the way I wanted it to.

I was introduced to a wonderful physician, Professor Gavin Marx, who is an oncologist working in Sydney. I shared Khun

Rotjana's story and the contents of the letter. The first thing he explained to me was that palliative care does not necessarily mean the end of life, it just means the patient is unlikely to be cured from their illness, which is quite different. He told me about a patient of his with a similar diagnosis to Khun Rotjana's whom he had been treating for many years. His patient could not hope for a cure, but under a careful medical regime could live a meaningful life.

There it was: the solution and evidence I was looking for. Khun Rotjana wasn't going to die, she just needed to be treated, and that treatment would continue for the rest of her life, but we weren't facing the end. The only problem here was this was my solution, not Khun Rojtana's.

With consent and agreement between Khun Rotjana and her treating doctors in Thailand, her medical records were given to Gavin and he conducted an assessment of the treatment she had received and the proposed health plan for her future treatment. His summary was that what the doctors proposed for her departed very little from what he would do given the same circumstances. Gavin advised one slight variation on one of the drugs prescribed, but that the treatment plan was sound and world class.

As the months passed I made many return trips to Thailand to spend time with Khun Rotjana, initially to offer her the good news of a positive medical intervention and then to plead with her to try the medical route that was on offer. But that was my plan and my choice, not hers. After the complications that she had experienced in her initial breast cancer treatment, which had left her with the most horrendous scarring, she refused to go down the chemo and radiation treatment path again. She had made her choice, and she made it clear to me that she would not entertain those options. Gavin often took my calls to discuss Khun Rotjana's health care, and provided wise counsel to help me accept that the decision was

Khun Rotjana's to make. I should support her, but ultimately I should respect her decision and wishes.

Some months later I ended one more bike ride at BTN to be greeted by her, this time sitting on a chair and supported by a metal-framed walker. I suspected it would be the last time. There was the loss of mobility and strength, the tiredness, and the gradual wasting away of her body. For those who have been part of the cancer journey of a loved one, I now share your pain. Since I wasn't living with Khun Rotjana, her decline was jarring each time I visited. Towards the end of the year, she became more unwell with each visit and I feared that each would be the last.

Late in November in 2017 I received word from Game that Khun Rotjana was in a sharp decline. I booked another flight to Bangkok and on to Phuket, arriving late in the evening. It was even later by the time I got to Baan Tharn Namchai. The next morning I travelled to the temple where Khun Rotjana was and sat beside her as she slept. I had only a few hours on the ground before returning to Bangkok for the evening flight back to Sydney once again. In the hours we spent together, she woke a number of times but seldom spoke. I felt content that I had arrived in time to see her, hold her hand and tell her I loved her.

As I was preparing to leave, Khun Rotjana became lucid enough to tell me she was ready. I thought she meant she had arrived at a place where she was ready to go. But I was wrong.

She was ready to take the course of treatment that included the chemo, radio therapy and whatever else was needed to keep her going. I was as shocked as I had been months before when I visited her at the Surat Thani Cancer Centre to learn that no one had told her what was wrong. Now, after months of rejecting the health care that was on offer, and after I had come to terms with respecting her wishes, she had decided to fight. I was on the phone to Gavin again, but this time I didn't need him to tell me the answer. It was too late. The cancer had spread too far, her body was too weak, the care that might have slowed or halted her decline could not bring her back now. It was too late for any of that.

I boarded the plane for another nine-hour flight back to Sydney, having been on the ground in Thailand for less than 24 hours, and as I sat there numbly all I could think was had I done enough? Had I done enough to encourage Khun Rotjana when she was well to give medicine a chance? It was a rhetorical question, of course, because clearly I had not. I was entrusted by those at the hospital and at BTN to deliver the news of the cancer's return. Was it not on me to push her harder? How can I face her daughter, knowing I might have done more to save her mum? Of course I respected her right to choose and to change her mind. But would things have been different if I had leant into the opportunity to influence her with more fight and passion?

That trip in November, as it turned out, was not the last time I would see her alive. The following month, together with Kay Spencer, now the chairman of *Hands* and a deeply trusted friend of Khun Rotjana's, I flew to Bangkok and travelled to the Bangkok Hospital in Phuket. Her room was full of people and it seemed to be meal time, which is all the time if you're Thai. Though her treating doctors confirmed that she was highly medicated and that her health had not improved, she was much more aware than on my previous visit. I'm glad I was granted one last opportunity to see her after that painful visit at the temple.

On Christmas Eve of December 2017 Khun Rotjana passed away.

I haven't yet found peace with how I supported Khun Rotjana through her decline. Was I showing respect for her wishes in the early days or was I avoiding what needed to be done? Her late change of mind raises the question, if a stronger influence had been exerted earlier, might she have come around to accept the medical care offered earlier, giving her a chance, or was this simply the way it was supposed to play out?

WHAT I HAVE LEARNED

People come into our lives for a reason, a season or a lifetime and we should embrace the time we have with them. Tell those you care about that you love them and never miss an opportunity to share a hug.

There is a saying that you die twice, once when your heart stops beating for the final time and again when your name is no longer spoken. If that is true, I can't imagine a day when Khun Rotjana will die a second time.

Khun Rotjana's presence at Baan Tharn Namchai will be forever missed. She *was* BTN for the decade or more it provided a home to the children who needed her care and love. But in her absence we move onward. It doesn't mean she will be forgotten; it just means we need to continue to move forward with her wisdom and loving example as our guiding light.

WHAT CAN YOU DO?

Enjoy what you do or change what you do, because we only get one go at this.

When we attach ourselves to one thing or one person and they are taken away, we may question our ability to live and love again. But loss is as much a part of life as birth.

CHAPTER 8
BELIEVE IN THE FUTURE

To be resilient is to know challenge and not be cowed by it. It is to stand firm in the face of adversity and to bounce back from misfortune. It is to adapt successfully to difficult or challenging life experiences. But without confronting challenging experiences, can we really claim to be resilient?

If resilience is the process and outcome of successfully adapting to challenging life experiences, then Mae Thiew has embodied a unique way of meeting those external and internal demands. I know of no one who has faced such daunting demands over such a sustained time yet has found a way to keep going in spite of the pressures.

For me, the key to resilience is dealing with challenges *over time*. One-off life crises, no matter their magnitude, are overcome by drawing on our skills and the support around us. It is when those challenges persist that we need true resilience.

I can rationalise to make sense of Mae Thiew's journey and even find answers to the question that I have asked myself so many times about her, which is: *how did she continue when there appeared to be no end to the challenges she faced?* When we believe the problem is insurmountable, we're probably right. When we hold on to hope and believe an end is in sight, again we're probably right. There is much to be said for the benefit of believing. But when the suffering continues for months, which turns into years and even decades, how can we possibly maintain hope? Perhaps we can say that we'll remain in the fight as long as our hopes remain stronger than our fears.

For as long as I have known her, Mae Thiew has battled stomach cancer. She has faced that battle in her own way, and her health ebbs and flows. I have seen her ride 1600 km over 16 days propelled by courage and determination alone. Yet I have witnessed her struggle to find the strength to walk 50 metres without the need to sit. But her health struggles are not what I think of most when I hold her out as a pillar of resilience. After all, she has a choice as to how she deals with those health challenges, but no choice as to whether or not she has them.

When we believe the problem is insurmountable, we're probably right. When we hold on to hope and believe an end is in sight, again we're probably right.

What I admire most and really do struggle to understand is how she continued to deal with the situation the children faced over such a sustained period of time. Because that she did have a choice about. At any point she could have simply given up and chosen to do something different. But she didn't.

Mae Thiew can appear hard, almost cold, and certainly untrusting, until she invites you into her life. I've already noted that I have found her in some ways to be quite unlike a lot of Thai people. In most settings I've learned to navigate the process by having a meeting before or after the actual meeting. This is so I can understand the true position, because asking someone to share their opinion in the presence of someone of supposedly higher social status is simply not going to work in Thailand. Saving face is of very real importance. Mae Thiew is different. She will not engage or humour you or agree to something because it seems like the right thing to say. Perhaps the formidable struggles she has endured over time have brought her to this place.

At the start, as knowledge of the work she was doing with the children born with HIV spread, so too did the demand, which quickly outstripped the funding she was able to generate to support the growing number of children in her care. HIV is no longer a medical problem and hasn't been for many years; it is a problem of poverty. Those living with the virus in developed countries can look forward to a normal life expectancy. Science and medicine have found solutions to this scourge, so long as you have access to the drugs, or the money to buy them. Mae Thiew had too little of both.

She had funding to care for the kids and provide medicine, just not enough for all of them, so inevitably some of the children were succumbing to treatable illnesses that ravaged their immune-deficient little bodies. As children became ill, then gravely ill, she was forced to decide who would receive the medicine they needed and who would not. She simply did not have enough to give to all of the children who needed it. She was effectively deciding who would live and who would die.

HIV is no longer a medical problem and hasn't been for many years; it is a problem of poverty.

This was not a struggle that existed during a few lean years — it lasted for decades.

Thailand is not a country that doesn't care for its own. In 2002 Prime Minister Thaksin Shinawatra introduced the country's first universal health care program that provided affordable health care for all Thais. Herein lay the problem for Mae Thiew. Because she was unable to prove the nationality of many of the kids, she was unable to access the public health care system. For these kids she was forced to turn to much more expensive private health care.

Mae Thiew was burying children who simply didn't need to die. There was a medical solution to their illness; the problem was access. How do you prove the identity of a child who had been abandoned at a bus shelter, left outside the local 7/11 or found on the steps of the police station? In all likelihood they were Thai-born, but without physical proof of their parentage how could you establish where these kids came from? Whether or not they were Thai, it was clear that access to medicine was a lifeline for these kids, and that for a price that could be secured.

Having made it my responsibility to research HIV treatments, I learned that death was no longer the prognosis for HIV sufferers. Indeed, they could now expect to live a relatively normal and productive life with a long life expectancy. All they needed was access to the necessary drugs. And therein lay the problem. The children at Baan Home Hug were dying not because HIV remained a medical problem but because of poverty. Those without access to the drugs died.

HIV is also a virus that builds resistance, finding a way to strengthen itself, if you go on and off the drug. So each time you go back onto the drugs they are a little less effective, meaning you need higher doses than before. For Mae Thiew, it wasn't as simple as deciding who would be the lucky ones and who would be cast aside. She did what she could for all of them, all the time. Each time she lost one of the children a little part of her died with them. It's no wonder, then, that her own body came to be ravaged by illness and poor health.

During those early years of my connection with Mae Thiew she would reveal the story of the home, the kids and her own journey like a Netflix series, with a new episode offered whenever I returned to Baan Home Hug. Each visit she revealed more, but not the full story. With each visit we built more trust and with the increased trust came more of the story. So every time I returned I earned a little more.

Her personal health journey is one few have an insight into. The daily struggle she endures is accompanied by a level of pain that few are aware of. She works hard to keep her personal emotions and struggles from the children, and her typical response when you enquire about her health is to raise her arms like Popeye and declare, 'I am strong!' I have found that I need to repeat the question three times before she will give me any real answer, but often it is a broad grin and a deep silence that gives the greatest insight. For a woman who exhibits such strength, her fears are very real and close to the surface, but are shared only with those who have earned her trust.

The question of how you continue in the face of endless suffering and adversity is uppermost in my mind whenever I think about the struggle she faced year after year in the two decades before our meeting. During one of my many visits to her home she shared with me that she had buried 1027 children over the decades she had been running Baan Home Hug. At the time it was simply too big a number to grapple with. It took me a long time to appreciate the frequency of loss that represented, and how death must have been such a common presence for the children. So the question I would ask myself was, how did she go on?

After the loss of the first 10, the first 50, the first 100, she must have asked herself, 'Is there ever an end to the suffering?' One thousand and twenty-seven, and she loved every one of them. Sometimes I see the pain in her and I know she carries a scar for every child to whom she has had to say goodbye.

There's no doubt that *Hands'* agreement to support her financially and provide what she needed for the children heralded a remarkable change. When they all started receiving life-saving medicines, complementary health services and regular nutritious meals, *the children stopped dying*.

Mae Thiew sees the meeting between us as 20 years in the making. She never let her fears outweigh her hope, but how did she maintain hope over that period of time, when surely she was entitled to think there was no change coming?

I think the resilience she demonstrated was based on a number of factors. First, to give up hope was to give up on the children. This was never an option for her. It was clear that the children mattered more to her than anything else.

Second, so long as she continued to care for the children there was the chance that someone who could help would step forward. If she closed the doors to her home, then there was nothing to step forward to. If there was the slightest chance that an answer existed somewhere in the future, she had to maintain a presence.

Third, she never allowed her thinking to be defined by yesterday or past events. She has an extraordinary ability to put the struggles of yesterday behind her and not let them define her tomorrow. Rather than focus on the growing number of children she had lost, her focus remained on those she could save. I can only imagine how debilitating it would be to do otherwise.

Fourth, doing something is always better than doing nothing. Doing what she could, even though the children were dying around her, allowed her to continue with the knowledge that she was doing all she could with what she had. When we give all we have without solving the problem, we can take comfort from knowing we have no more to give.

Doing something is always better than doing nothing.

Finally, I believe her strength, resolve and hope were mirrored in the children. Knowing her strength gave even those who were losing their battle resolve and courage, which was reason enough for her to continue her struggle.

There was nothing special in what we did at *Hands* other than removing the barriers to empower Mae Thiew and her team to do what they had been doing for decades. The saddest part was not that the children had died, but that they need not have. The medicine that would have sustained them was available, to those who had money. What we contributed was to make people who had the capacity aware of the children and their needs.

We didn't use images of dying children in our marketing campaigns to evoke pity or emotion. We simply invited people to join us on a bike ride and meet the kids for themselves to remove any fear, stigma and preconceptions and just allow people to see how these kids deserved a chance. They deserved to be well and healthy, to be acknowledged and to be loved. They needed to know they mattered.

While Mae Thiew's resilience equipped her to meet, adapt and respond to the challenges she faced, I came to understand that perhaps her biggest worry was in the challenge she couldn't address — her own mortality.

Trust is a beautiful thing. I have built it and (I'm ashamed to admit) broken it at different times in my life, for I am filled with imperfections. But what I have been able to give Mae Thiew is reason to believe we care for what matters most to her, the children. Her greatest fear is what will happen when she is no longer around to care for the children. Who will care for them, who will provide for them, look out for them and love them as she does? And it's not only the kids in her direct care that she worries about. Kids who have left Baan Home Hug to make their own way in life have a way of returning at different times. Some return to visit, to work or to bring gifts of bags of rice. Some return because they are sick, and where else should they go when sick but home. Mae Thiew's door is always open. Occasionally kids who are terribly sick will return to a place of safety for their final days, knowing they will be loved without judgement. Who can provide that in her absence?

At *Hands* we do all we can to provide for both staff and kids across the homes we support. We provide certainty around income, we provide guidance and support to our directors, and at every opportunity we advocate for the rights and futures of the children. Through our work we contribute to the UN's 17 Sustainable Development Goals. We celebrate when kids leave our homes to be reunited with families. We celebrate when they graduate from university and find their way in life, and we celebrate their moving on to live a life of choice.

But I have no answer for Mae Thiew on who will replace her. I know this is her deepest worry and fear and that it permeates through her staff. They too worry that when Mae Thiew passes our support will stop, that we are there only for her.

During a trip to Baan Home Hug before COVID I sat down with each of the staff to hear how they were, how we could better support them and what they needed from us. Over the course of several hours I heard the same message from the accountant, the cook, the driver and the rest of the team. They appreciated all we did, but feared our support would end with the passing of Mae Thiew.

I was surprised that after more than a decade of uninterrupted support such a fear persisted in either Mae Thiew or the staff. Returning to Australia after that trip, I spent a good part of the nine-hour flight from Bangkok back to Sydney troubled by their fears. What more could we do to convince them of our commitment to them, not just in the good times but in the bad too.

Embrace authentic optimism rather than false or cruel optimism.

I have to trust that we will be as fortunate as we were in replacing Khun Rotjana at Baan Tharn Namchai with someone who cares equally about the kids there. Whoever it is will not be Mae Thiew, as Game is not Khun Rotjana. They will be different, and that's okay.

One of the things that I believe has allowed Mae Thiew to meet all the challenges over such a long time is her embrace of authentic optimism rather than false or cruel optimism. For her, authentic optimism is acknowledging what she has to deal with, the resources at her disposal and whom she can call on to assist. It is accepting her ability to bring about the change she can. Cruel optimism would be to tell her staff and the kids that everything was going to be okay, that soon they would have all the help they need. It is the difference between truth and unrealistic hope.

Accepting what is in front of us and working to change that by whatever means we have is more constructive than simply hoping for something better or different, without changing what we do. Hope is not a plan.

I have spent countless hours since 2011 riding next to Mae Thiew on one of the many bike rides we have shared. Riding with Mae Thiew is always an interesting experience. It is a conversation shared through osmosis rather than active participation. Her English was very limited in the early days, and none of the riders spoke enough Thai to do anything other than greet her with respect. She would ride each leg of 25 km and then seemingly spend the entire water stop in deep recovery before she would repeat it all again.

Those who ride with her are always inspired by her resilience, her ability to get back up, point that wheel down the road and ride another leg when you might expect that she had no more to give. Knowing her story and seeing her courage, commitment and determination certainly lifts all of those around her.

....

Accepting what is in front of us and working to change that by whatever means we have is more constructive than simply hoping for something better or different, without changing what we do. Hope is not a plan.

....

She would often take dinner in her room as she recovered for the next day. But this in no way took away from the experience—it just seemed to add to what we were sharing with her. When she was diagnosed with terminal cancer, years before I met her, she was given limited time to live. She rejected western medicine after seeing her father die from the same disease. She was determined she wouldn't go the way he did.

As a riding group, knowing of the medical challenges that Mae Thiew rode with, we felt privileged to be in her company on the journey. For us, these bike rides are so much more than that. We describe them as 'memorable shared experiences', but that hardly does them justice either. I have heard them described as 'life-changing' and numerous variations, one of my favourites being 'chicken soup for my soul'.

WHAT I HAVE LEARNED

What I have learned most from my deep connection with Mae Thiew is the boost for both body and spirit in finding and embracing something you care deeply about. The renowned thought leader Seth Godin once said, 'The challenge of our time is to find a journey worthy of your heart and your soul.' I have watched the way cancer has attacked her body and how she is able to rebound from these painful episodes. Is it the potions she mixes, the fresh exotic fruits she eats or the storied power of Tiger Balm? I think not. Seeing her health rise and fall over so many years, how many times have I left Baan Home Hug wondering if I would see her again, only for her to rebound magnificently. The only thing I can attribute it to is the power of her connection to the journey, which is food for her heart and soul. It is the benefit of believing.

Whenever I am asked to talk about resilience my thoughts turn to Mae Thiew. Regardless of the company I am talking with, the challenges they face, the path they have travelled or the road ahead, I can't help but think of the challenges she has faced and the resolve she has demonstrated. After more than a decade of sharing her journey, I attribute her resilience to five things. First, she has a deep connection to and belief in her cause, which is the children she cares for above and beyond all else. Second, her continued presence and care for the children created the opportunity for someone to support what she had achieved. If she had closed the doors, there would have been nothing for *Hands* to support. Third, she is able to put the struggles of yesterday behind her and not let them define her tomorrow. Fourth, she understands that doing something is always better than doing nothing. And fifth, the strength and courage with which she responds to her own personal challenges offers an example to the children, who mirror that strength and courage.

WHAT CAN YOU DO?

In building a stronger resolve in yourself and your team, think about how you can learn from the past but focus on the future. The future is where hope lies, not in the past. You can ensure that your hopes are greater than your fears by continuing to take action and move forward. You might not have the solution in your sights, but you are getting closer.

CHAPTER 9
FIND CLARITY THROUGH ACTION

If we do nothing, then nothing will change. Beset by adversity and uncertainty, we may fear taking action. When what we know to be true no longer is, the paralysis of inaction can be more comfortable than the dread of action and uncertainty. But often the only way to get to the other side of our biggest challenges is to forge right through them, and that starts with action. When we are held back by uncertainly, action can lead us to a place of clarity. The more we do, the clearer things will become.

In less than three months, between the beginning of January and mid March 2020, I had led two bike rides for *Hands* and was feeling that the true joy of riding in Thailand had been lost somehow. Looking ahead in my diary I saw that we had another four corporate rides to lead. It was beginning to feel a bit like a job rather than the pleasure it had always been. When choice morphs into obligation, it's funny the feelings that can manifest.

Often the only way to get to the other side of our biggest challenges is to forge right through them, and that starts with action.

The year 2020 had started the way 2019 had ended, with flames and smoke and deep concern for our farm and our stock. Claire and I would spend day after 40°-plus day clearing anything combustible from around our farm in the Capertee Valley west of the Blue Mountains in New South Wales. The years of drought had wiped out a lot of pasture and what remained was dry grass that crackled under your feet.

In normal times, the only light we would see out of our bedroom window at night was the endless stars of the night sky. But over the summer of 2019–20 we watched the eerie glow as the fires burned their way along and slowly down the escarpment, and we thanked our lucky stars that the fire had not reached our property. The fires had started in October of 2019 and as we approached the end of another year they were growing in intensity.

Come the new year and we had to decide which of us would travel to Thailand to lead the ride and which would stay and protect the house and the stock. We couldn't both go and leave the farm and animals on their own, and we couldn't both abandon the obligation we had to the ride and to *Hands*.

The exploding canopies of surrounding gum trees frequently reminded us of the intensity of the fires in the valley around our farm. It had been three months since the start of the Gospers Mountain fire and our first rushed trip from our home in Sydney to the farm to gather up the photo albums and other irreplaceables. For three months the fires that burned around and along the ridgelines seemed to get steadily closer. As the days passed, more and more communities up and down the east coast of New South Wales were first threatened and then consumed by fire, and as the fire marched closer to our farm it built in intensity.

Every day we worked on the farm and around the house, clearing gutters and sheds, preparing emergency water sources to fight the fire and each night moving the cattle into a paddock close to the house to give us the best chance of protecting them should the fire reach our boundary. We took comfort that if it came from the south, we had a chance. It would travel through cleared paddocks, and if the drought had gifted us anything it was paddocks free of grass— good for reducing the fuel for fire, if not great for feeding stock. What grass remained in the paddocks was now tinder dry and would take very little to ignite and race from paddock to paddock. But at least with the fire hoses and water sources we felt we had a chance.

Any fire from the west and we had no chance. The property next to ours is 300 acres of native bush and scrubland, and to make matters worse the topography of the land is such that the highest point is our boundary, so a fire from that direction would be basically unstoppable as it raced up the hill towards our boundary fence and house.

Claire and I didn't manage to see in the new year. We were in bed well before midnight, exhausted from another 40-degree day preparing for what might be coming. We had agreed that I would stay at the farm and Claire would fly out to Thailand the next day. On January 1 she drove to Sydney and I headed for the Capertee Rural Fire Service shed for a briefing on what we could expect. They laid out their plans and briefed us on their mitigation efforts and how their resources would be deployed. I left feeling confident that this collective group of exhausted men and women had done all they could to protect their homes and those of their neighbours. It felt like there wasn't much else that could be done.

I left the fire shed and drove the 18 kilometres back to our property. It seemed a longer drive than usual, as I was very conscious that the further I drove the further I was from assistance. Finally I drove over the cattle grid at the highest point on our property and pulled the car to a stop. For the first time I could see the flames leaping 10 and 20 metres in the sky in the south-west. From what I could tell they had to be on my neighbour's property.

I continued to monitor and refresh the RFS Fires Near Me app, which was providing the most up-to-date information on the progress of the fires. I knew from the briefing that the road back to Capertee would be closed, and the app now showed that the road out from our property in the opposite direction was also closed.

I was stuck on the property, and unless there were fire teams inside the road closures no one was coming to help. The flames were bigger and closer than at any time during the previous three months. Whatever happened next it was going to be up me, and Burton of course. Happy New Year and welcome to 2020, I thought wryly. If only I had known what a shitshow 2020 would become.

More than once I would stare out at the flames and challenge them. 'If you're coming then let's get this over with, I'm ready as I'll ever be.' Then I'd see another explosion of dark grey smoke in the tree canopy not far away and be happy they hadn't. The air was full of burning gum leaves carried by the hot winds. I knew it would take only one of them to ignite the dry grass on which they fell and all hell would break loose. For the next couple of days the routine was the same. Wake and be grateful that I hadn't been woken during the night by the smoke alarm signalling that the house was burning. I'd check that Burton was next to me on his bed and that was as good a start to the day as I could hope for.

....

Happy new year and welcome to 2020, I thought wryly. If only I had known what a shitshow 2020 would become.

....

I'd hand feed the cattle, all too conscious of our diminishing feed stocks, and release them into the paddock, then go about any other chores that might contribute to the protection of our home and stock. The RFS called on me to offer assistance, along with the Head Government Vet who was touring properties to check the welfare of stock. Both gave me the thumbs up and wished me luck with whatever came our way.

The days were not without distraction and bright moments. One morning, while Claire was leading the ride down Thailand's east coast, I walked out to feed and release the cattle to welcome in a new calf. No matter what, the circle of life would continue.

That afternoon helicopters flew directly over our farm on a mission to save the Wollemi Pines, also known as the dinosaur trees, which are found within the Capertee Valley that we call home. The helis were flying at low altitude and sourcing water from dams on neighbouring properties to attack the fires that threatened these highly endangered trees. As a helicopter pilot myself I was content to sit on the veranda watching the pilots manoeuvre their aircraft through dense smoke and imagine the conditions in the hot cabins reeking of smoke. I admired the skill and dedication of the aircrew and was happy to sit this one out.

By now Claire was riding through the Isan Region of Thailand along the banks of the Mekong River, something we had been doing together since 2013. It was certainly a strange time, and the first time since 2009 that I had not started the year on my bike in Thailand surrounded by amazing and inspiring people.

As the group travelled south I could tell from the rare occasions that Claire and I were able to speak on the phone that while her body was in Thailand, her head and heart were back in the Valley, but change was a-coming.

A few days into the new year I woke to a noticeable drop in the temperature; the change we had all been hoping for had arrived. Rather than waking in a lather of sweat to a temperature in the thirties, the morning was cool and pleasant. The sky wasn't filled with the rising sun, but instead there was a delightful cover of cloud, not formed from the accumulation of smoke, but those wonderful nimbostratus clouds that bring rain that hangs around for hours and days.

The rain that began to fall would eventually not only extinguish the fires but yield an end to the drought that had brought many farmers to their knees and the brink of financial collapse. Even the newborn calf was doing well. Reassured by the long-range weather forecast and the end to the fires I felt comfortable enough to leave the farm and head to Thailand.

Tens if not hundreds of thousands of people have their own stories to tell of the 2019–20 fires. Many lives were lost and homes and properties destroyed. Having suffered no measurable loss, our dance with the devil was hardly worth talking about. However, I reflect on the times that the fire reached our boundary and the outcome was less than certain, and I believe I found comfort in action.

I don't know that our preparatory efforts would have made a difference, particularly if the fire came from the west, but I do know that each night when we finally lay our heads on the pillow we felt we had done all we could that day and we knew we would do more the next. Being willing to confront challenges in life without knowing the answers or, sometimes, even the questions optimises our chances of meeting and overcoming the challenges. We are always better positioned by doing something than by doing nothing.

I landed in Thailand to join the end of the ride, and while it wasn't the start of the year or the ride preparation I would have liked, there was comfort in sweating it out on the bike on the roads of Thailand, watching the weather back home deliver day after day of welcomed rain.

Being willing to confront challenges in life without knowing the answers or, sometimes, even the questions optimises our chances of meeting and overcoming the challenges. We are always better positioned by doing something than by doing nothing.

Within weeks of finishing the January ride and returning to Australia I would be back leading one of our corporate groups from New Zealand as they rode down the Andaman coastline of southern Thailand to Baan Tharn Namchai. I returned immediately to Sydney and had a couple of domestic trips to speak at conferences before returning to Thailand within the week for other work commitments. While I was on a return flight to Sydney via Singapore, Claire was on QF23 out of Sydney heading to Bangkok; 2020 was shaping up to be a massive year of exciting projects, travel and living out of a suitcase. Well, so I thought.

It was shaping up to be our biggest and best year on several fronts. We had six rides confirmed for the year with 200 riders paid up and all the fundraising done. We would exceed all prior fundraising goals and we had three incredibly exciting projects on the go that were ramping up for delivery that year.

For the past couple of years leading up to 2020 I had begun to feel that some of the drive and enjoyment in leading *Hands* had left me. The rides hadn't been the fun they used to be, the fundraising was a burden and I was increasingly questioning if I should still be involved in *Hands*, and if so in what capacity. Was I delivering value? For a while I had felt the spark had left me and what had become monthly trips to Thailand were more tiring than exciting.

The fundraising I had been doing in some capacity for the previous 15 years was wearing thin and the responsibility seemed to be sitting more heavily on me. Personally and professionally I was exhausted. I was not delivering the best of me, and I was wondering where the change would come from.

I often find myself in conversation with people who have experienced an event in their life to which they have responded by starting a charity. When asked, my response is always the same. Starting is easy—perhaps too easy; it is continuing when you are heavily relied upon that is the hardest part. Finding someone to take over the responsibilities you have created isn't easy, because these responsibilities aren't always attractive to others.

The previous year, 2019, had created exciting new opportunities for *Hands*, however. I saw a chance to move *Hands* to a new level and bring a new level of support and growth to the children and communities we were working with. There were three new projects that offered particular challenge, and all at once I was back where I loved to be—overwhelmed and fighting my way forward.

The first new project to present itself was building a Digital Learning Centre. Back in 2014 I had travelled to Pittsburgh in the US to spend time with Bill Strickland, the founder and CEO of the Manchester Bidwell Corporation. This was a man whom I had admired from afar, given the philosophy he had applied to addressing socioeconomic problems firstly within his home city of Pittsburgh and then across the US. Basically, his approach can be summarised as providing education that leads to employment rather than education for the sake of gaining a qualification. During my time with Bill I realised the sense in his approach. They were educating members of the community for whom traditional learning environments didn't work, and he realised that if he partnered with local industry and commerce and identified resource gaps, they could train their students in the educational areas needed. They were educating not for qualifications per se but for jobs.

All at once I was back where I loved to be—overwhelmed and fighting my way forward.

When you think about how much of the content of a university degree is directly applicable to a specific vocational role and how much of it is there to make up the credits necessary, it made sense. Returning from my time in Pittsburgh with Bill and his team, I knew that his model was directly relatable to the communities we were working with in Thailand. It wouldn't replace the formal education offered by university or technical colleges, but that clearly wasn't for everyone either.

Through 2018 and 2019 we explored the delivery of skills-based learning to our older kids and those living in communities outside of the homes we supported in Thailand. Long before work from home became the norm and part of the mix for how so many of us fill our week, we identified there was a market for the delivery of remote services, particularly in the digital services industry.

We chose Baan Home Hug, in the town of Yasothon in the northeast of Thailand, as the centre where we would build a Digital Learning Centre and deliver training that would lead directly to the employment of the kids and members of this regional area. The benefit was that it was introducing a new industry to this area of Thailand. It would create new employment opportunities, which would offer higher incomes, directly leading to improved standards of living. And the most attractive part of it all was that it allowed these kids to remain in the community in which they had grown up, at least until they decided to leave. Rather than finishing school with limited opportunities outside of Bangkok, this gave them choice and a future they could control.

We started working with both Apple and Deloitte, who were enthusiastic in their support. We started working with a tech provider, Diakrit out of Bangkok, who were also totally on board. We secured funding to build a state-of-the-art Digital Learning Centre with multi-use capabilities. The first sod was turned in mid 2019.

The second project was an obvious one given our location and the infrastructure we already had. The southern area of Thailand stretching from Pang Nga down to Phuket is dominated by international tourism and the market that supports it. The biggest employer is the hotel and hospitality sector, and even before COVID the biggest challenge they faced was attracting staff. They didn't have to be good; they just had to be there.

We set about surveying the key decision makers of the top and mid-tier hotels from Phuket to Khao Lak with a series of questions, one of which was, 'If we ran a hospitality training centre in Baan Nam Khem, would you be likely to employ our students upon completion of their training?' The response from the general managers and HR managers who participated in the survey was a resounding yes. What's more, our survey prompted a number of direct approaches from hotels wanting to be partners in what we were creating.

In creating the hospitality training centre we already had the building. In 2011 we had built a tsunami refuge centre containing 13 individual rooms with their own bathrooms, training rooms, a commercial kitchen and even a front desk that could be used by students as a simulated reception area. Only minimal capital investment would be required to make it fit for purpose.

I travelled throughout Asia looking at other similar operations to learn from those already in the space. The more people I spoke with, the more opportunities presented for us to partner with those already operating in this space, and the more value we realised it would bring, particularly to the communities in the southern area where tourism and hospitality was at the core of their livelihoods.

Rather than duplicate what was already offered by other providers, our unique point of difference was to fill a gap for those in the community for whom formal multi-year education wasn't right at that point. Of course we recognised the value of the university and technical college programs, but what we were looking to create was a pathway for those who had never thought that formal education was an option. If we first gave them training that would lead to better employment opportunities than were currently available for them, then perhaps more formal training leading to recognised qualifications would follow. The first step was to expand what they saw as their limited choices.

As the model for the Hospitality Training Centre started to take shape, Scott Stein, a *Hands* director, and I visited other centres in Vietnam, and we came to the same conclusion. This could work, and it was exciting. Scott had also visited Bill Strickland's centre in Pittsburgh, so he too grasped the model.

Then we received an offer, which to be honest I just didn't know what to do with. The local Thai government reached out to Game, the director of Baan Tharn Namchai, to offer us a disused school that had closed due to low attendance numbers. The school was located in a small farming community about 15 minutes' drive inland from the resort area of Khao Lak.

Game and I drove from Baan Than Namchai to Khao Lak before heading inland. My first visit to Khao Lak was in the days after the tsunami of 2004, when the landscape was very different from what I was seeing now. In early 2005 the view was defined by destroyed buildings and abandoned cars, the whole landscape covered by mud and sand that had been picked up by the advancing wall of water and deposited over the entire coastline, and the salt water carried inland killed much of the lush green vegetation native to this area.

The terrain we now drove through as we headed to the village seemed pristine and untouched. There were towering palm trees and vines that reached towards the thick forest canopy. I have walked the Kokoda Track a couple of times and had a sense of being back in the jungle, only here I was only 15 minutes' drive from the beautiful coastline of Khao Lak dotted with swimming pools and resorts.

Past tiny market gardens and modest homes we arrived at the long-abandoned school and I was immediately inspired by the beauty of the setting. Steep mountains rose to the south of the road that led us in, and circling the school to the north, creating a natural boundary, was a fast-flowing river that filled the air with the sound of cascading water. It was hard to believe that this idyllic place was only a short drive from the five-star hotels of Khao Lak. I was immediately drawn to it but had no idea what we could do with it.

Wandering through the ramshackle buildings, I feared that even the most optimistic renovator might have struggled with the challenge. Several buildings were arranged in an L shape. I could imagine the distraction of sitting in class as a student, with this beautiful river and the looming mountains covered in jungle-like forest on the other.

Walking from classroom to classroom I could see the potential. Between the row of classrooms and the road were sports fields, long overgrown, but it was these and the way the mountains seemed to create a natural theatre that gave me the inspiration.

I thought about what *Hands* had done and what we provided for the kids and communities we supported. We had built homes for kids living in unsafe environments, provided access to medicine and health care for kids who suffered from HIV, and ensured they had access to both secondary and tertiary education. I considered what the kids had access to in Thailand through our homes and the support of our generous community. Something was missing, and it suddenly occurred to me that sport might be the game-changer.

As I stood in the school grounds I thought of the potential of creating a sports academy that offered development opportunities, and not just for our kids or those from the Khao Lak region. If we did it properly, we could attract kids from across Thailand, who would fund places for those who might otherwise be unable to attend.

Between the row of classrooms and the road were sports fields, long overgrown, but it was these and the way the mountains seemed to create a natural theatre that gave me the inspiration.

I imagined building a centre that not only offered high-level sports training but could be used by corporate groups travelling to this area for conferences, retreats and wellness programs. There was certainly nothing in the southern area of Thailand, or to my knowledge anywhere in the country, catering to those needs in the way I envisaged.

What surprised me about the High Performance Sports Academy concept was how well it was received. I reached out to a number of leading sports stars, including the captain of the Australian men's cricket team, and there was strong interest from all. I was used to putting forward some pretty left-field ideas that took some convincing, but what I was getting back was keen interest and strong endorsement from the outset.

The Digital Learning Centre and the Hospitality Training Centre either were funded or required little capital investment to realise them. It was just a case of doing the work, and all of us at *Hands* were up for that. The sports academy was a different story. It was going to take some serious investment to get it off the ground and to do it in such a way that it would attract foreign corporates and leadership teams as a destination of choice for their off-sites and wellness retreats. Having spent the past eight to ten years at *Hands* raising money to maintain the relatively modest status quo, the idea of setting a multimillion-dollar target above and beyond our recurrent funds appealed to me. I believed that with the credibility we had in delivering life-changing and indeed life-saving programs, we could do it.

The final endorsement, if I needed any, came during a two-day trip to Thailand to visit our projects with a senior partner from Deloitte Thailand. The relationship between *Hands* and Deloitte had grown with their support of the kids through the Digital Learning Centre. We met in Phuket and travelled to our sites in Khao Lak. We visited our original home at Baan Tharn Namchai and the rubber plantation that we own as a means of generating sustainable income, and I took him to Baan Nam Khem. After lunch I said, 'I have one more site I'd like to show you on the way back to the airport.' His reaction so far had been encouraging but not rapturous. I had doubts that anything he had seen was all that exciting to him, and driving towards the abandoned school I wondered if it was worth the trip and how he would receive the sports academy idea.

I hadn't spoken about it on the drive other than to say I had just one more potential project and we would swing by as it wasn't out of the way. When we arrived at the school he had a similar reaction to mine on my first visit. Really, it's hard not to be inspired by the picture-perfect setting. We walked through the classrooms and towards the soccer fields. We stood in the middle of the soccer fields with the mountains behind us looking back to the building and I then shared the concept of the sports academy.

If he had been lukewarm or had shown no more than polite encouragement for our projects so far, that tepid reaction was gone now. As I laid it out the concept of a sports academy offering sports facilities and programs that would also cater for executives as a retreat, he responded with unbridled enthusiasm. I knew then we were on a winner and that raising the $5 million to $10 million I anticipated we would need would be a challenge but not an unrealistic one, and it would take us to the next level. I returned to Australia with my mind spinning with the potential before us.

Friday the 13th of March 2020 is my Black Friday. I had not long landed back in Sydney after that exciting trip when things changed and changed quickly. COVID-19 had arrived. I could see its potential to impact the way we did things in the charity.

Claire was leading the Digital Live Ride to the temple at Wat Yan Yao for what was always an incredibly emotive reflection session before the final three kilometres of their 500 km journey from Hua Hin that had started five days before.

I was days away from leading a corporate group of our supporters from NARTA, who have been with us since 2007, along the Milford Track in New Zealand. We had 20 executives ready to walk the track in support of *Hands*. All their flights and accommodation were booked. At around 10.30 am I received a phone call from NARTA CEO Michael Jackson, who expressed his concerns about COVID and whether we would even be able to fly into New Zealand. The tour to New Zealand would need to be postponed until things settled down. Not cancelled, he assured me, just postponed.

While I was on the phone with Michael I could see that the CEO of Business Blueprint, Dale Beaumont, was also calling. Each year he led a group of business owners on a five-day, 500 km ride across Thailand in support of *Hands*. They had been riding with us since 2013, had raised well over $2 million and were due to ride within 10 days. I called Dale back and we discussed the situation and agreed to defer the ride until September, because surely everything would be back to normal by then, right!

It wasn't yet lunchtime when I received the third and final call that would break my spirit that day. The owners of a property development group out of Melbourne OYOB had been riding with us for many years, and they were due to ride in a few weeks' time, just as the Blueprint Ride was finishing. That ride was postponed too—we finally ran it in July of 2022. The Milford Track walk would never happen.

The first challenge was in the cancellation and notification of all involved. Thankfully the entire *Hands* community who were to trek or cycle with us were incredibly understanding and patient as we worked through the logistics. None of us anticipated just how long-lasting the impact of the pandemic would be. Adopting what he saw as an abundance of caution, Dale wanted to hold the cancelled March ride in September of 2020; it would be September 2022 before we could host the riders in Thailand.

The challenges we faced were of course not unique to us. Everyone has their own stories about the impact of the pandemic from both a personal and professional perspective. Some industries, such as those involved in anything to do with home entertainment or home improvement, actually thrived, enjoying some of their best sales on record. Others involved in travel and hospitality, not so much. The effect varied widely in the charity sector too. Some of the big charities enjoyed growth, while we would lose 75 per cent of our projected income over the two proceeding reporting years.

The greater challenge for us was that our recurring costs in keeping the homes open, the kids fed and cared for, and the staff in jobs didn't change. We couldn't reduce the number of staff in our homes and we couldn't make any significant cost reductions, yet the model on which we had built *Hands* couldn't work. For the foreseeable future we weren't able to run our international bike rides or host our Future of Leadership conference series.

Claire returned from Thailand and avoided mandatory hotel quarantine by just a few days. She joined me at the farm, which became our sanctuary during the lockdowns. We could tend to the cattle and horses and breathe the fresh air, all while complying with the stricter lockdowns that were becoming the norm.

We would survive COVID and the massive disruption to our fundraising, though there were certainly casualties along the way. We would lose our Australian team, with the exception of Claire and Jenny Tuntevski, who manages our books and finances. We couldn't keep an events person on the team when we were no longer able to host events. It's difficult to justify a sales role when we had no events to sell, and the marketing agency became a luxury that we couldn't afford.

We survived because we had good savings in the bank to ensure there would be no disruption to services when the unforeseen occurred. We also managed to host a number of new events that did generate income. The biggest source of funds was our most valued supporters at NARTA and the members and suppliers who make up that buying group. Without NARTA's support, I'm not sure we would have made it through.

The additional challenge we faced was the long tail of COVID. The two rides that were due to occur in March 2020 and were eventually held in July and September of 2022 were all paid up, and the fundraising done for 2020. So when we delivered the ride in 2022 there was very little 'new' income. They were riding on the credit of the fundraising that had been undertaken in the lead-up to their 2020 ride, with most of the funds raised during 2019.

The other casualty was the programs we were set to deliver. The Digital Learning Centre came to a halt as the disruption to business experienced by our partners at the time had them focused on their adjustment to the challenges they were experiencing. The Hospitality Centre project was shelved, to be pulled back out when circumstances changed. As for the sports academy, my fear is that we had had a window and that window has closed.

The following year, 2023, has seen us return to the rides and generate new income through our fundraising. However, our first ride of the year, in January, was still a deferred ride from 2021 and the legacy issues of fundraising undertaken in previous years were attached to that. We also had to deal with the increased cost of the rides that had been quoted on two years before. We didn't feel it right to go back to the riders and ask for more money. COVID just continued to give.

WHAT I HAVE LEARNED

If you do nothing, then nothing will change. From the cleaning of the burnt leaves that fell to the ground on our farm during the fires to the events we hosted during COVID, some hugely successful, some less so, the important thing was to keep taking action. Should the charity have not survived during the years of COVID we might have been criticised for not preventing it, and that would have been warranted. But we could never have been justifiably criticised for not trying.

The other learning that was reinforced for me was that if you give people information you will often get their understanding. During COVID our board was forced to approve the use of a percentage of donors' funds to sustain our ever-shrinking team here in Australia.

For 11 years we had operated on the promise that 100 per cent of funds raised went directly to the homes and kids we support. We were proud of that promise and our community certainly appreciated it. But in 2020 we wrote to our community to advise that the board had agreed that for a two-year period it might be necessary to change that position. Hand on heart, I can say the *only* feedback we received from the community was sympathetic and positive. There may very well have been negative feelings or responses to the communication, but we didn't hear about them. A good number of our donors actually *increased* their contributions.

You don't have to win each and every challenge you face, but you will win support by facing up to the challenges.

WHAT CAN YOU DO?

In the challenges you face in life—both those you see coming and those that sneak up on you—you don't have to have all of the answers. It is more than okay to ask for help and to admit to those who are looking to you for the answers that you just don't have them.

Consider the challenges you have faced or are facing and the pressure on you to solve them. Where is the majority of the pressure really coming from? In my view, it is likely that the internal pressure you put on yourself exceeds the external expectations of others.

Find a way to be kind to yourself, to give yourself the space and latitude you likely give others confronting similar circumstances.

Finally, be kind to others, because we just don't know the depth of the shit that others are dealing with and how all-consuming for them that can often be.

PART III

THE
VISIONARIES

These are the dreamers, but not in their sleep; they are fully conscious and mindful when they dream and then set about pursuing those dreams. They don't let the past define them or wallow in what might have been; rather, they spend time in opportunity. They understand that not every endeavour will be achieved, but that nothing will be achieved without purpose and effort.

Our visionaries create a legacy that seldom centres on them, because rarely is it about them. The true visionary doesn't just imagine what can be, but creates a pathway for the leaders and achievers to follow. And on their journey they will pause to feed their soul, knowing that we achieve most when we engage the heart, head and hands.

CHAPTER 10
FIND A JOURNEY THAT FEEDS YOUR SOUL

I believe the challenge of our time is, as Seth Godin puts it, to 'find a journey worthy of your heart and soul'. We live in a time when, for the overwhelming majority of us, our essential needs are met. We have access to nutritious food, safe and comfortable accommodation and an increasingly high standard of living, with more people travelling abroad than any previous generation, yet the incidence of mental illness grows at alarming rates. I will leave those working within the sector to decide whether this is a result of a rise in numbers of those suffering mental health issues or a reduction in the stigma attached to mental illness and more reporting around it, or a combination of both. Regardless, as a society we have a problem, and it is not going away. How much this is a problem for 'society' to solve and how much it comes down to the personal responsibility of each of us to do more to meet our needs is an open question.

The challenge, or journey as may be, is to find what feeds your soul and invest in that. It need not be ground-breaking, scary or pushing your limits, but it does need to be pursued with integrity because it is what matters to you and not about the image of you it creates. It's the thing you do when no one is looking, when it is not captured and shared with the world who will assess you as an individual in 0.6 of a second before moving on. While it might not need to be on the edge of our physical limits, I do believe that our greatest achievements are often accomplished when we were about to give up but continue in spite of the struggle.

After speaking at a conference I will often engage with members of the audience who want to chat, sometimes to ask a question they prefer to keep private, sometimes to share a personal experience they believe will resonate, sometimes simply to thank me for the presentation. Then there will be the person who shares with me their desire to do what I have done. That might be setting up a charity, leading bicycle tours in Thailand or creating a life that feeds their soul. The challenge I routinely put to my audiences is this: 'When was the last time you did something that was food for your soul? Not for your husband, your wife, your partner or your kids, but for you?' For me, a big part of it is the shared experience. But clearly that's not so for everyone. Whatever it is, the important thing is to find something that is not measured by the likes or follows of your favourite social media platform, but by the feeling you get when you're alone.

'When was the last time you did something that was food for your soul?'

Sometimes that magic happens not when you have engineered it but when you've simply created a space for it to happen. I have ridden my bike in Thailand since 2009, covering either 500 km or 800 km each time, and as the years have progressed these rides have taken place multiple times each year. I reckon I have clocked up conservatively 25 000 km on my bicycle on the roads of Thailand. I have led both public and private rides through parts of Thailand that few get to experience. Speaking to many Thai nationals both in Thailand and abroad, and sharing my travels in their country, the overwhelming majority have never visited the places I have been.

Each ride is different and each delivers nuggets of goodness. From cruising along deserted roads under the shade of towering palm trees to darting through the back streets of villages, there are always good times to be had pushing pedals. Without a doubt your body undergoes a chemical response when you exert yourself physically that ensures pleasure follows pain. I will always find pleasure in riding my bike, whether it's a gentle, serene, meditative experience or a full-on, no-holds-barred sprint, but much of the joy and the food for my soul comes from watching others have their own experiences.

On a post-COVID ride in 2023, I rode with a mum who told me that hearing about our rides at a conference where I had presented many years before she had sworn she would 'one day do that ride', but for many years the time wasn't right; there was always a reason to put it off, to put the needs of others before her own. I wondered how much the demands that she endured as a health professional during the global pandemic helped to bring clarity that there was never going to be a 'right time' to do the ride, unless she decided to make it happen.

Cycling had never been part of her life and as a busy working mum her personal needs were the last to be met, which is the case for too many mums. Committing to do the ride was an audacious move, not just to prepare to ride 800 kilometres in eight days but also to take on the fundraising that is an essential part of our program.

If you were to set key performance indicators to measure the success of such an undertaking, what would they be? They would probably include getting home safe, enjoying the ride, finishing the ride in one piece, and of course making a difference to the lives of the kids who are a big part of the reason why we all ride in Thailand. But what of the personal, life-changing experiences and outcomes you simply never saw coming?

Tracey was riding with us for the first time and was feeling all the anxiety and apprehension of the first-timer, which dissipates only after spending time on the bike. That's part of the reason why we structure the ride the way we do. Four days of riding, followed by a rest day then another four days of riding. The first four days allows everyone to rid themselves of the anxiety and find their place in the group, and to appreciate that no one gets left behind.

The rest day gives time for a massage and to get ready for the final four days on the bike. The final four days allows the riders to relax, to enjoy the pleasure of cycling and to appreciate the beauty of the country we are riding through, and to enjoy the company of those we are sharing the journey with. Many of the riders I talk to before the end of the first ride signed up believing they were doing something for someone else; they wanted, to use that overused cliché, 'to give something back'. That is the mindset they arrive with, but they all leave with an appreciation of how rich their lives are and what the ride has given them.

During the first four days of riding Trace had been in the van for a number of legs, opting to take some time off the bike. Before she arrived in Thailand she might have been disappointed, feeling she had failed in some way. On the night of the fourth day I spoke with her about her journey so far.

Trace had ridden 70 km that day. It wasn't the entire day, but it was well beyond the furthest she had ever ridden before. She told me she had learned a number of things that day. I asked her to share her biggest learning with me. She explained that while she was here her sons were in Canada skiing. Normally on a ski trip Trace had been happy to sit it out and watch. However, on the back of her riding in Thailand and the newfound confidence she had gained from doing what she and probably others thought was beyond her, she had decided that she wasn't sitting life out anymore. She called her boys to tell them what she was doing, what it meant to her and the place that she had arrived at, and that from now on she would be on the ski fields with them. She wasn't going to sit in the cafe and dutifully wait for them. No more sitting on the sidelines. The response from the boys was to say how proud they were of her.

I could have packed up and finished then and there. It is these magic moments, these real gifts that come when we decide to engage in life rather than finding reasons to sit it out or wait for the time to be right, because surely as we sit on the sidelines waiting for our turn, someone else is taking theirs.

Dan Pallotta, a charity founder and thought leader in the charity space, has said, 'People are tired of being asked to do the least they can possibly do, people are yearning to measure the full distance of their potential for causes they care about deeply.'

It is my experience that the charity sector can and does offer unique opportunities for people to take the full measure of their potential, and if they care deeply about the cause, that is a bonus but not a necessity.

Starting a charity to support children left without families in the aftermath of a global disaster will enjoy strong initial support and interest, but there is an expiry date on that compassion. For many years the focus at *Hands* has been on seeking first and foremost to provide value to those who engage with us, rather than simply seeking donations. The positive change is not limited to the kids in our homes or the Thai communities we support; it also affects those who support us. If we can provide opportunities for outcomes like Tracey's, then we know we have created positive change among our supporters too.

I could have packed up and finished then and there. It is these magic moments, these real gifts that come when we decide to engage in life rather than finding reasons to sit it out or wait for the time to be right, because surely as we sit on the sidelines waiting for our turn, someone else is taking theirs.

Dan Pallotta is absolutely right: people are tired of simply being asked for donations. When we can create a true value exchange, when our supporters, our riders, believe they have received more benefit than they have given in the exchange, then we are providing that opportunity for people to feed their soul.

How do you know when what you are doing is feeding your soul? I think a really good measure is when it is hard to articulate to others, when you are filled with a sense of gratitude. When you truly appreciate the benefits of the experience, then you're likely feeding your soul.

At *Hands* three-quarters of those who ride come back and ride again. We have a higher number of riders who have ridden four times or more than those who have ridden between two and four times. What that tells me is the ride is meeting a need, it is the conduit that our community is looking for when it comes to meaningful experiences and feeding the soul.

Of course our rides appeal to a relatively small audience. The importance here is to find what it is that leaves you struggling to articulate its benefits for you. Deep inside of you there is something so incredibly important that you're drawn back to it time after time, finding a way to overcome the obstacles that may prevent you from participating. It is that important to find a way to make it work.

Before I look at the key ways the rides feed my soul I want to share the reasons people give for holding back.

The biggest reasons I hear from people who, when expressing a desire to join us, follow it with that *but*: 'I could never ride that far' or 'I could never raise that amount of money'. If they genuinely believe either to be true, then they are probably right. More often than not, when people tell themselves something is true and believe it to be true, then it is. If they believe they can do it, they do; if they believe they can't, they won't. In those early discussions I don't try to convince them, but if they are open to the conversation, if it is fear rather than belief, then we have something to work with and can address their concerns and fears. With fears we can bring logic, process and a proven way to address their concerns based on what we know has worked well in the past.

More often than not, when people tell themselves something is true and believe it to be true, then it is. If they believe they can do it, they do; if they believe they can't, they won't.

The next biggest obstacle to people pursuing something for themselves is the perception that they are too busy and don't have time. Again, if they are unwilling to look for opportunities to bring change into their lives, then they are simply giving greater priority to everything else rather than creating the space to invest in themselves.

We know that a healthy diet is good for us. We know that regular exercise is equally good for us. I would happily make the case that taking time to feed our soul is equally good for us on so many levels. In a society that is struggling to deal with an epidemic of mental health issues, surely there will come a time when we accept that investing time in feeding our soul is valuable preventative care and good for our mental health. Someone who regularly and actively pursues an activity that feeds their soul, I suggest, is better equipped to deal with the pressures of life.

So what are the moments, the feelings, that bring me back to Thailand to ride my bike again and again? How is it that, after leading more than 30 rides, I still finish each one feeling nourished and in a better place than when I started? I have identified 10 ways in which the ride grounds me, brings clarity and sets me up for months ahead.

THE PEOPLE

This is an easy one for me. Given that I am an introvert, you might find it surprising that it is at the top of my list, but it is a clear winner. The people who join our rides have made a substantial investment to be a part of it. They made a commitment many months before the ride itself. The training needed to prepare for the ride will have been substantial. The necessary financial commitment, once airfares are covered, approaches $5000, then of course there is the fundraising, which is a challenge in its own right. All of this means the rider who is less than 100 per cent committed simply won't make it to the start line. This ensures we have a group of people who have invested in themselves and each other. But it is not just the other riders we will spend 14 hours a day with; it is also the people we interact with along the way.

Thailand is known as the 'Land of Smiles' for a reason. As in nowhere else I have ever travelled, the typical first response from a Thai is one of warmth and friendliness. Riding through the villages and communities along the way we are greeted by all sorts of people going about their business. They welcome us with a smile. It is hard not to enjoy yourself when you are constantly met by 'Hello' or '*Sawadee Krap*' as you cycle past. The motorists, whether on motorcycles or in large trucks, all respond with courtesy, giving you room to pass safely.

THE CHANCE TO SUPPORT OTHERS

From the rider's perspective, supporting others is more about the riders they share the journey with than the higher purpose of raising funds to support the kids. For me, one of the highlights of every ride is the contribution the participants make both individually and as a group to getting all of the riders through. Success doesn't necessarily mean riding every leg but ensuring that the ride is a hugely beneficial and impactful experience for them.

When people are physically and emotionally challenged, pretence can be stripped away and honesty revealed. You see and experience true human emotions of gratitude and appreciation.

The opportunity to improve someone's day or a particular leg on the bike takes many forms. It is amazing the energy paradigms you can pass through over an eight-day ride. There will be extreme highs and there will be days when you wish the whole ride was over. But each extreme passes, and the presence and support of the rest of the group will help reduce the struggle. Maybe someone rides up to you and starts a conversation, about something that is important or simply amusing. A talking point that can last a good 45 minutes and get you through to the next water stop, where you arrive grateful for the company and the distraction. Or it may be simply acknowledging that what we are going through is tough but that's okay. Tough can be good or it may mean extending a hand and giving a rider a wee push up a hill.

When people are physically and emotionally challenged, pretence can be stripped away and honesty revealed. You see and experience true human emotions of gratitude and appreciation. You help someone who truly appreciates the support and expresses their gratitude. It is a delightful exchange to be a part of.

THE 'TRACEY MOMENT'

Supporting others requires your active participation in the experience; you're in the game as opposed to being an observer. The 'Tracey moment' occurs without your participation; you're just fortunate to be a witness to what has occurred. It is a gift I cherish, but not every ride will deliver something as profound as the 'Tracey moment'.

On a pre-COVID ride I was leading a ride for a corporate group from New Zealand. There were 60 of us on the road, and I tried to spend time with each of the riders over the three days. Many highlights emerged from that ride, but one was shared by a mum of teenage kids. She told me her family didn't engage in a lot of organised sport or physical activity, so signing up for the ride was a huge deal for her. She was racked by doubts, even as to her ability to make the start line. But before starting she first had to start riding.

At first it meant time away from the family as she headed out to train. Then the kids started riding with her, and before she made it to Thailand the training had become a shared experience with her kids that had now become a regular part of their lives. It had gifted to her and her kids something that in all likelihood they would not otherwise have shared. Now they were riding regularly together and were sharing both the health benefits and more time as a family. Rather than the training taking her away from her kids, it brought them closer together.

I have heard many such stories of people who previously weren't riders returning home with a newfound passion for cycling. Whether they continue to ride when they get home is a personal choice, but what they discover on the ride is a determination to no longer sit out life, but to actively participate. That is a huge gift, not only for themselves but for those of us who witness it.

> *Whether they continue to ride when they get home is a personal choice, but what they discover on the ride is a determination to no longer sit out life, but to actively participate.*

TIME TO THINK

The ride gives you time to think, although come day seven as we gather for our last dinner together you will wonder where the time went and how quickly those eight days passed. We spend, on average, five hours a day actually cycling. The day starts when we push off at 7 am, but when you factor in our water stops and lunch stop and other unanticipated breaks along the way, we normally pull into the hotel between 2 and 3 each afternoon. If we are averaging 100 km per day, then each leg between water stops is between 20 and 25 km long, which is around an hour to an hour and a quarter in duration. So for between four and a half and five hours a day you are in command of your bicycle and your thoughts.

Time on the bike gives me time to think. I often use it to plan the year ahead. I run through a checklist in my head of what I want to do both from a work perspective and in my home life. I also find myself reviewing the past 12 months and appreciating the good with a desire to correct the bad.

THE MEDITATIVE STATE OF RIDING

I love the meditative element of physical activity, which comes easily when you have trained, for example as a runner, a rider or a swimmer. You know the feeling, when you invoke a 'Forrest Gump' state, feeling as though you could just keep on going. This meditative state takes over when you are riding with a fair degree of pace and effort, your legs, pedals and tyres rotating in perfect rhythm. You are 'in the zone'. I know I am in this space when I look at my Garmin and wish the water stop was further away, so the state I am in could just continue. It's not that I am deep in thought, just that I don't want the space I am in to stop.

You are riding with a fair degree of pace and effort, your legs, pedals and tyres rotating in perfect rhythm. You are 'in the zone'.

THE PHYSICAL EXERTION

I enjoy those particular legs where, either on your own or, best, with others, you find yourself going full gas for as long as you can, until you reach the next water stop or simply have no more to give and sit up in the saddle. The thing I love about these legs on the bike is that they are very rarely planned or contrived. We just seem to find ourselves towards or at the front of the pack. Those who choose to participate will start to put a few bike lengths between them and those riding at leisure.

The pace will start to build, the formation of the group will take shape, the chat will stop and the riding becomes intense. From here on you are riding with all you've got. Your legs will be screaming at you to stop, and you're praying for the next rider to take their turn at the front. It's painful but also joyous. The thing that makes these legs so much fun is that the hard work is something you choose. I find there's pleasure to be had from a hard session that ends with a sore body. It's as though your body is acknowledging the effort and reminding you of the gains you have made.

THE PHYSICAL ENVIRONMENT

Immersing yourself in nature and all that it has to offer—the physical elements, the sights, sounds and smells—further enriches the experience. When exploring a destination, cycling gives you a perfect vantage point and speed, quicker than walking or running, allowing you to cover more ground, but much slower than a car so you have plenty of time to take in the scenery.

Our rides in Thailand are planned so that more than 90 per cent of the route is off busy roads. On our northern ride we cycle along the banks of the Mekong River, which separates the countries of Thailand and Laos. The ride takes us through rice fields, tobacco plantations, market gardens, fields of lemongrass, cassava and pineapples. The southern ride follows the coast of first the Gulf of Thailand and the Andaman Sea. Each ride offers something very different in landscape and riding conditions. The southern ride has rolling undulations while the northern ride is predominantly flat.

The changes and unpredictability of the weather, in my mind, only adds to the experience. Riding in the warm rain of Thailand can be a refreshing and joyful experience. Waking up to the sound of rain on the roof, knowing that you soon have to get on your bike, is less so, but it is only uncomfortable until it is no longer.

THE SHARING

Sharing the experience can mean riding next to one another, or against one another on a hard leg, or sharing the evening meal, but one of the highlights for me each ride is the sharing that occurs a couple of kilometres from the end of the ride. On the last day, with only a few kilometres to go, we pause to share our individual experiences of the ride. We sit in a group, and each rider takes their turn to share what have been their high, low and grateful moments during the tour. The only rule is they must have to have a response for each—saying 'I didn't have a low' is unacceptable.

The power of the moment is in the sharing by all of the riders. It is a beautiful experience to be part of. By this stage of the tour there is no need to pretend to be something you're not or to hide your emotions. This is when we hear the 'Tracey moments' that might not yet have been shared, the personal experiences and the magic that is really only understood by those who have been part of the ride. The timing is by design. I can't think of another point on or after the ride when there would be greater willingness as a group to be so vulnerable and authentic. The emotions are real.

They are not fuelled by alcohol but are as raw as people will get in the context of a safe and supportive group of people who only eight days before didn't know each other. For me, this is a highlight of the tour, but you need to have experienced the ride and all it offered to be entitled to share in the vulnerability and honesty the session summons.

THE GOOD THAT COMES

It should be evident by now that there are many layers to the ride. Everyone will take away their own personal experience, something unique to them and their journey. There are the relationships that are built, the memories that will live with you forever, and of course the knowledge that while we are all having this deeply immersive, life-changing experience, it is also bringing significant and meaningful change to a group of disadvantaged children.

Depending on the size of the group, each ride will raise between $100 000 and $500 000. This brings enormous benefit to the charity, making a very real difference to what we can offer the children. It allows us to pay the staff and provide medical care for the children. And it ensures that those who have a desire to go to university can do so without the burden of a debt at the end of their studies, to pursue a life of choice not chance.

By the end of the journey the riders have seen the balance shift until they clearly feel they have taken more from the ride than they have given. Therein lies the food for the soul.

Knowing the good our riders bring to the communities we support in Thailand allows them to sign up without feeling they are doing it only for themselves, which in some strange way they might struggle to justify. By the end of the journey the riders have seen the balance shift until they clearly feel they have taken more from the ride than they have given. Therein lies the food for the soul.

THE END OF THE RIDE

On the last ride I did while writing this book two Thai boys from the home we were riding towards rode with us. We always have some of the older kids or staff join us for each of the rides as a way of enriching their lives and bringing a connection to the home and those we support to the ride. Those who ride with us are selected by the director of the home in recognition of how they have chosen to live their life at the home, setting a good example for the other kids and working hard at school, and it is something they want to do.

The two boys with us this time left an indelible impression on all of us. The older of the two boys, A-Chi, was sad to see the ride come to an end, such was the journey he had had. He was clearly riding slower and willing the ride to keep going. The other boy, Cha, was excited to be heading home to see his best mate and the other kids. He missed his family. The closer we got to home, the faster he rode, so he was breaking away from the group as we got closer.

Close to the end we are all filled with contradictory feelings. You can't wait to get to your destination and see the kids you have ridden to support, but you don't want this amazing journey to end. Dismounting from the bike for the last time, you embrace your family and friends who have travelled to meet you at the end of the ride. It is a chance to share one last sweaty hug with your fellow riders and time to reflect on the journey and its purpose. Emotions are as mixed as the participants. Many lack the words to articulate how they feel and what it means to them. It is special beyond words, understood only by those who have made the journey, and without question food for the soul.

WHAT I HAVE LEARNED

Taking time to find what feeds your soul, then investing in that, is good not just for you and for your overall mental and physical health, but for your family and for your colleagues. If you find something that engages your hands, head and heart, you are heading in the right direction, but it's not something you can do once and expect it to sustain you. For me, it's a bit like running a marathon. The high will come on race day with the rewards from the work you have put in to get to the start line. But the physical benefits of the run will last only so long. If you don't keep running after the event, the physical benefits will steadily diminish. We need to continually carve out time to invest in ourselves. It is not selfish to do these things; quite the contrary, it is selfish not to. To be the best version of ourselves for those we love the most, we need to invest in us, not at their expense but for their benefit as much as ours.

WHAT CAN YOU DO?

First, accept that investing in yourself is not a selfish pursuit, that it is as much for those you love the most as it is for you. Remember the 'Tracey moment' and how the ride inspired her to live a bigger life with her sons, no longer as an observer, and the boys will reap as much from this learning as will she.

Try different things until you find your thing and your tribe. It doesn't have to be what your husband, wife, partner or mates enjoy. Find what it is for *you*. When it invokes a feeling of gratitude, then you may just have found what feeds your soul.

CHAPTER 11
ENGAGE HEART, HEAD AND HANDS

In his wonderful book *Stolen Focus: Why You Can't Pay Attention*, Johan Hari explores the impact that our connection to devices and social media has on our ability to form meaningful relationships. Our relationships, be they professional or personal, are built on the back of shared experiences. The depth of those relationships is often enhanced when the experiences challenge us. Physical, mental and soulful challenges lead to the deepest relationships. We create meaningful experiences by seeking out opportunities to engage the heart, the head and the hands.

Back in the day, when the streetlights came on, it signalled it was time to head home because dinner wouldn't be far away. Now, what child doesn't have a mobile phone in their pocket or more likely in their hand, and if they are off with their mates, mum or dad can track their whereabouts using an app. Not that society has become more dangerous to warrant this. We haven't seen an explosion in kids getting grabbed off the street by strangers never to be seen again. Crime statistics suggest the opposite: we are far safer outside our homes now than in decades past.

We create meaningful experiences by seeking out opportunities to engage the heart, the head and the hands.

Why, then, are we increasingly fearful and overprotective as a society? Childhood obesity is a greater risk than random kidnappings. We serve our kids better when we teach them how to deal with stuff going wrong, how to stand up after a fall and carry on. Telling them they better not run or they might fall teaches our kids not to try and that it would be safer to sit this one out.

In recent years I have taken up the sport of ultra-marathon trail running. It's a sport that takes me into the bush to run distances of 50 to 100 km. I am pathetically slow and without grace or technique, but I somehow find my way to the finish line. I will set off at 7 am and will still be running, or walking as the case may be, 8 to 20 hours later as I cross the finish line. There's no good reason for me to have taken this on. My job doesn't require it, it's not an essential life skill, and there are moments in every race when I asked myself, 'What the fuck are you doing this for?' Then, in the final five kilometres, the end gets closer and the music at the finish line is louder. Crossing the finish line is an incredibly euphoric experience.

I see that same level of elation and wonderment at the finish of our 500, 800 or 1600 km bike rides in Thailand—particularly, but not only, in those undertaking the ride for the first time. The concept behind our rides originated in 2008 when Brigid

Gibson, who worked for CommBank in Australia, announced to her husband Andrew that she planned to ride a pushbike from Bangkok to Khao Lak to raise $10 000 for *Hands*. He said, 'Brig, I love you but that isn't one of your smartest ideas. Let's just make a donation of $10 000.' Thankfully for us, Brig ignored Andrew and set about planning to ride from Bangkok to our first home at Baan Tharn Namchai, a distance of around 800 km. Brig reached out to me to seek my blessing. I asked if I might join her and she was quick to welcome me into the peloton of two!

That first year, 2009, we had 17 riders: my kids, my dad, my partner and a dozen other friends signed up, and Gill, with whom I had originally set up *Hands*, flew out to join us. There was never a thought that it would be something we would repeat — that is, not until we finished the ride and I reflected on the experience we had shared.

I remember sitting at the hotel on our first morning applying sunscreen and worrying about my ability to ride that far. What if I couldn't keep up with the others? Would I make it through the first day, and could I possibly complete *eight days* of riding? It wasn't as though I had come prepared — I didn't even own a bike that year.

As I said, my three kids joined me on that first ride. At the time Lachie was 15, Kelsey was 13 and Jack had turned 11 just weeks before. I spent the entire time riding with one of them while the other two were on the road further ahead. If I was riding with Jack, Kels and Lachie would be further up the road in the company of other adults, some of whom they had met only days before. The kids might have come on that first tour for the novelty and excitement, but one of my greatest joys has been riding with them over the years since, when they have elected, first as older teenagers then as young adults, to come back and ride.

After the success of those early rides, in 2011 we started running 'the double', which meant I rode 800 km from Bangkok to Khao Lak, had two days off, then flew back to Bangkok and rode another 800 km with another group. In 2012 we changed the route, introducing the Isan Ride, which started in the far northeast of the country just outside Udon Thani, and for the next seven and a half days saw us ride along the banks of the Mekong River that separates Laos from Thailand. This route is radically different from the Coastal Ride, not just for the landscape but for the people and villages we encounter along the way.

A decade on from our first one in 2009, we were leading multiple rides each year. Our public rides in January were open to anyone and everyone; our private or corporate rides were held throughout the year. The 2020 season would have been our biggest year, with 200 confirmed, registered and paid-up riders over six rides. The growth of our rides wasn't owed to connections within the cycling community; it was through connecting with people who were looking for a shared experience, and joining us just meant they had to ride!

Our two main sources of recruitment are those who have ridden with us before and become our advocates and those who hear me talking about the rides at a conference, and it speaks to them as a challenge they are up for. I will often have people approach me after a presentation and talk about how much they would love to do the ride, but either the fundraising or the riding is beyond them. I seldom believe them on either score, knowing it is their limiting beliefs that hold them back more than the challenge of the ride or the fundraising itself.

I have completed more than 30 rides in Thailand, each of 500 or 800 km, and I'll admit that not every day of every ride has been a joyful experience, but there's not a ride I haven't enjoyed. What makes them so special are the people I share the journey with.

What builds the bonds and friendships is the shared struggle and the support along the way, from a gentle hand on the back of a struggling rider to the wordless companionship that says, 'You've got this—we've got this.'

A ride I led in 2018 for a New Zealand business came off the back of a previous corporate ride in which the managing director of this business took part. It was just after lunch on the first day when Mark rode up to me and said, 'Bainesy, do you think you could do this for my company?' Twelve months later he arrived for a three-day ride from Bangkok to Kanchanaburi. A number of things were stacked against the 2018 ride. Mark had all but made the ride compulsory for his 60-odd staff, for a good number of whom I'm sure, if they had been free to make their own decision, riding a bike for the first time in many years for one hundred kilometres a day in the heat of a Thai summer was not something they would have chosen. It was pretty much the hottest time of the year and to top it off they arrived at the hotel at midnight on the night before the first day on the bike, which equated to 6 am New Zealand time, after a long 24 hours of travel.

The first leg of the first day would reveal plenty.

Too many of the riders really shouldn't have been there. They lacked any training or even a base level of fitness that can substitute for training. It was hot and after the first 25 kilometres I was concerned at just how slow the pace was.

What builds the bonds and friendships is the shared struggle and the support along the way, from a gentle hand on the back of a struggling rider to the wordless companionship that says, 'You've got this—we've got this.'

Thankfully, we had a bus that followed the riding group and at each water stop more riders were stepping away from their bike into the air-conditioned comfort of the bus. Which wouldn't necessarily have been a bad thing, except that when it was time to get back on the bike at the next water stop, fewer got off the bus than got on! By the end of the first day one rider was being treated in hospital for a combination of exhaustion, dehydration and heatstroke. As the tour group headed out for dinner that evening Mark headed to the hospital with the disquieting feeling that he had made a mistake, that maybe this was beyond this group.

The next two days were like the first, without the trip to hospital but with the bus getting fuller at each stop. The final leg of any ride is probably the easiest. We float into the home to visit the kids and share a meal knowing that tomorrow we don't have to rise, don the Lycra and get back on the bike. On this occasion we enjoyed a wonderful evening by the River Kwai, most famous for the atrocities that occurred there during the Second World War. The following morning, before an afternoon departure from the hotel, we gathered all of the riders for a reflection session, a chance for the riders to talk about their journey and what they took from it.

When I entered the room that morning to facilitate the discussion I expected that it might not be pretty and that there could be some damning comments about the ride, the experience and those who organised it.

Well, you could have knocked me down with a feather. One after another the riders spoke about their experience, without any reference to how much time they may have spent in the bus. They spoke about the love they had for the company, the respect and admiration they had for Mark in having the courage to take on the ride, and how deeply connected they felt with their colleagues, some of whom they had not met until three days before at Auckland airport.

As the discussion continued to unfold in the room that morning Mark looked more and more like a proud father whose tough love was being repaid. We spoke afterwards about the feeling, the honesty and the connection in the room that morning and how it had exceeded all he could have hoped for. We both acknowledged that without the challenge of the first couple of days the results would not have been so dramatic.

···

They spoke about the love they had for the company, the respect and admiration they had for Mark in having the courage to take on the ride, and how deeply connected they felt with their colleagues, some of whom they had not met until three days before at Auckland airport.

···

So did the outcome of the ride translate into a better business for Mark and the company he led? Well, he brought them back in 2020 and we rode again. This time they had more time on the ground, and the engagement and connection through shared experience was even greater than on the initial ride.

In 2018 I spoke at a conference that was part of a development program in the real estate industry and was the brain child of Steve Carroll. Steve, who came from a tech background, brought smart people together to assist real estate agents in embracing new systems and processes. The program was called Digital Live and Steve didn't start it as a side hustle to generate new income for himself; he started it to assist the industry and commit the profits to an Australian-based charity working to support kids and communities in Australia. As the program was never about building wealth for himself the proceeds from the program weren't huge, but they amounted to several thousand dollars, which was gifted to a large, well-known charity. The experience with the charity turned out to be less than ideal and for a charity with a budget running in the hundreds of millions of dollars a donation of $5000 wasn't going to change a lot.

Speaking at the conference, I shared stories of the work I have done on a global level, including the bike rides. My presentation closed the conference. Within five minutes Steve approached Claire and said he'd like to send three or four people on one of our rides. Of course she said they would be welcome.

Within a week Claire, who used to work with Steve, had proposed to him that they run their own ride. Within another week we launched the first Digital Live Bike Ride in Thailand. Steve quickly amassed 23 riders from across Australia and New Zealand to be part of the first industry bike ride. These were super-competitive people who were coming together for the greater good. But to give up a week of their time, fly out to Thailand and ride 500 km over five days, there had to be more in play than simply feeling good, and Steve could see the benefits very early on in the ride.

On day three of the ride he rode up to Claire, who was leading the ride for *Hands*, and said, 'Do you think we can do two of these rides next year?' The interesting part of the timing of Steve's question was that it really had nothing to do with the kids or the homes we support. He had no greater insight into the lives of the kids or their needs on day three than he had when he launched the ride. He hadn't visited one of the homes. He was simply seeing what we know is the power of the rides. When you create these memorable shared experiences, people build relationships that they wouldn't otherwise, and business people naturally like to do business with people they like.

This ride included not just agents and those involved in the listing and selling of properties but suppliers to those agents and business owners, people doing business with the agents. For them, the ride became a gold mine of future business opportunities. Forget about the 30-minute sales meeting. The riders had hours and days to get to know one another, and from there business was done. One of the suppliers started the ride with 70 per cent market share of the riders; he left the ride with 100 per cent market share for his particular product. The product itself didn't change over those five days, but his relationship with his clients did, because they became friends who had shared something special.

When you create these memorable shared experiences, people build relationships that they wouldn't otherwise, and business people naturally like to do business with people they like.

But it's not all about bikes, business or even the kids in Thailand. A late inclusion on one of the 2020 rides was one rider's daughter, who had recently broken up with her boyfriend and found herself in a world of pain and with time on her hands. It was suggested that she join him on the ride. Sounds like a great idea, but you won't have an easy time of it riding 500 km over five days without the opportunity to get some practice time in the saddle. You can be match fit all you like, but unless your bum has been on a bike seat, you will be in for a hard time of it.

No surprise, then, that she found herself in misery and torment at the end of one of the long days. There were tears and likely an unspoken desire to be anywhere other than in that hotel room knowing that tomorrow she would have to get up and do it all again. So what does a dad do when he sees his little girl hurting? Well, he wants to fix it and right there and then. 'Would you like a cuddle?' and slowly she nodded in the affirmative, and her dad lay down beside her, dried her tears and let her crawl up and put her head on his shoulder, taking them both back to a time when she was a little girl. She fell asleep in her dad's arms that night. Recounting the story later, he said it was the first time in some 10 years that had happened. No matter the outcome of the ride, how many kilometres ridden, how much money raised, that night there was enough reason to ride. It created an opportunity for a father and daughter to share an experience, one that neither will forget. Right there they were banking memories that will serve them both well in the decades to come.

The real estate crew were back riding in 2022 at the first opportunity after the borders opened, and finishing that ride they set about planning future rides. Without a doubt there is a personal satisfaction and fulfilment to be derived from the ride. It is grounding, it is food for your soul and it gives you a healthy dose of perspective. The ride forces you to consider your own health and fitness and creates an opportunity to spend more time doing something for yourself.

I myself rack up multiple personal benefits from time on the bike. I enjoy the conversations. I enjoy watching first-time riders transition through fear and self-doubt to a newfound respect for themselves and their ability. I enjoy the early mornings as we leave the hotel with the sun climbing above the horizon, and the peace and tranquillity of that first leg of the day. Equally, I enjoy the hard legs on the road where I am sweating like a champion and desperate to make that water stop for food and fuel, but happy to have punished my body for the past 20 or 30 kilometres because

I know the pain will be gone in a few minutes and I'll be glad to have pushed hard. But I can't go past the finish of the ride, not because I have completed the distance, and there is actually a touch of sadness and regret that another ride is over, but for the delight of watching the riders, particularly the first-timers, process their own experience. For some it will be an overt celebration, for some the finish can be overwhelming and challenging in itself, for others it will prompt deeper reflections.

Whatever their individual response, the riders have changed and are different people now. Speaking with riders from the 2022 rides, a recurrent theme among the returning riders was that 2022 was their most enjoyable ride. Many had ridden several times before, but 2022 was something special. It's safe to say that for most of us, before the global pandemic we took a lot of things for granted. Few of us had experienced the loss of choice, the loss of freedom and the loss of income we did during those two and a half years of lockdown. We came out of that with a new sense of appreciation, a recognition that we shouldn't take our privileges for granted, and that we really need to enjoy the moments and seasons rather than wishing and waiting for something different.

Considering the learnings to be taken from meaningful shared experiences, I think there is a direct correlation between effort and reward. The greater the effort, the greater the reward. Our bike rides attract people who are predominantly not bike riders. Go figure! People sign up to ride 800 km and it is not a passion for cycling that attracts them. Renee, who has been riding with us since 2011 and has completed seven rides, doesn't even own a bike and is not particularly fond of cycling. What she loves is the immersive experience of spending nine days on tour with an amazing group of people who come from diverse backgrounds but have enough in common to bind the group.

It starts when they make the commitment, which can be an impulsive act after a keynote or a more gradual, deliberate decision. For Claire and Tracey, our 2023 riding nurses, it took 11 years to finally commit. Some need time to get their life in order. Signing up for the ride is a big step, but that doesn't put you on the plane to Thailand.

Our bike rides attract people who are predominantly not bike riders. Go figure!

Committing to a fundraising goal of between $5000 and $20 000, depending on what ride you are undertaking, is also a major step. Again, through experience I know that the fundraising is achievable and is important, not just for *Hands* and the kids we support, but because it fundamentally shapes the rider's experience. Setting, striving for and ultimately reaching the fundraising target earns the rider a deserved sensed of entitlement from the start. It also helps them to frame the ride as the 'reward' for their fundraising success. With the support of the team at *Hands* each of the riders will develop their own strategy for raising their funds. What works for one person might not work for the next, and even those without corporate networks or big social networks can raise their funds. It is often a case of strategising and exploring ideas with our Fundraising Manager and then implementing them over the months in the lead-up to the ride.

Arriving in Thailand for the ride for the first time nonetheless is usually accompanied by a huge sense of anxiety. No matter the briefings, the videos or the information sheets we provide, the same questions remain: Will I be able to ride that far? Can I keep up? What if I'm the slowest? Is it going to be too hot or hilly? After the first couple of days we see the riders settle into the groove and find their spot, and the anxiety of the first day is left on the road behind them. They come to understand that someone will always be the slowest, and that's okay. They learn that we celebrate the arrival of each rider at each water stop and each lunch break, and the loudest cheers are reserved for the back riders on the last leg of each day. We have no prizes for the fastest riders or the first up the hill. We embrace those riders who are openly there for each other, those who build individual strength and confidence through the group's achievements.

This individual growth in confidence is one of the greatest products of the ride, and that growth is based on trust.

From the weekend warriors who ride with their mates for a hit-out followed by coffee and trash talking through to the pros riding in the famous Tour de France, cycling is very much a team sport. Sure, one of the greatest joys of the sport is that whenever you feel the itch you can quickly don the lycra, slip into the cleats and helmet, and there will be a roadway that awaits. But anyone who has ever ridden at more than 25 km/h then slipped in behind another rider knows the benefit of riding with a mate, working together to reach the destination faster and with less effort than if riding alone. If you still have doubts, simply watch the closing stages of a professional road race where the peloton chases down a breakaway rider. Seldom does the single rider stand a chance of holding off the chasing pack. Working together, the riders in the pack take turns at the front, breaking the wind, those sitting behind enjoying a brief respite before taking their turn at the front, until another rider eases ahead of them, and all the while the breakaway rider is on their own, with no respite and no sharing the energy of the group.

Our rides in Thailand couldn't be further removed from the professional rides of the pro tour, yet the same principles apply. When we work together as a team, taking turns to push into the wind, drawing on the energy of the group, we achieve so much more than would be possible on our own. Many times I have ridden beside one of our riders and been thanked for getting them through the leg. Often we just ride next to each other in silence. The mere presence of someone alongside you during challenging times inspires you to keep going. The only thing that really changes for you is the conversation inside your head, which shifts from 'I'm going to stop and get in the van' to 'I'm supported now and I know I can go further'.

The building of trust within a team happens over time. The greater the challenge the team faces, the more the journey towards the building of trust and unity is expedited. It doesn't mean that everyone starting out on the journey will end in perfect unity, but it helps to arrive at the place of knowing sooner. Are you aligned with our goals and direction? It's not about bending and conforming until you fit. Sometimes deciding this is not your tribe, these are not your people, is the best outcome for all.

The mere presence of someone alongside you during challenging times inspires you to keep going.

If you leave with clarity around what didn't feel right, that will help you on the journey to finding what is right and will create a space for someone else to step into. Leaving a job, a career, a relationship or a marriage can be and often is bloody hard and messy. But staying for fear of change and of being true to yourself denies you and those involved a sense of true belonging and self-worth.

Our rides in Thailand bring together people of all shapes and sizes from different vocations and circumstances who would have had little likelihood of crossing paths but for the ride, and herein lies the magic. When we meet on the first night for the welcome drinks and the presentation of jerseys, without question assumptions are made. The typical leading questions, of course, 'Where are you from?' and 'What do you do?' shape those assumptions.

A friend of mine, Paul Watkins, is a business owner, pharmacist, ultra athlete, keynote speaker, author, property developer, forklift driver, mountaineer, adventurer, husband and stay-at-home dad. He describes how he is judged by those he speaks with depending on which role he is performing at the time. If he leads with, 'I have twice participated in one of the toughest foot races on the planet, the 6633 Arctic Ultra—a 583-kilometre unsupported solo race deep into the Arctic Circle. The first time I failed to complete the run and recorded a DNF. The second attempt I won it, becoming the first Australian to do so,' you can bet that generates greater interest than if I lead with, 'I'm a stay-at-home dad'. Just for the record, Paul is too humble to lead with the first, and values the second role as far more challenging than the first. But we are conditioned to size people up based on appearances, ask a few clarifying questions then put them in a bucket.

But there is little time to do that before the ride starts. What we find is that we are all dressed in the same riding kit, we are all riding the same brand and type of bike, and we are all riding in support of the same cause. The job you do at home and your financial status become less important. The ride strips away individual ego as it becomes about supporting one another. There is no 'race' either—the win is in lifting everyone up. The speed of the group is determined by the amount of support the slower rider receives. We enjoy more time in the pool or soaking in the ocean after the day's ride based on our mutual support rather than on the speed of the quickest rider.

The confidence and competence built from the back of the bike seat ultimately leads to increased trust within the group. The riders, who days before had not even met each other, now find themselves riding wheel to wheel, charging the front riders with the safety of the entire group based on good communication and trust.

If the front riders don't communicate to those riding behind them the hazards on the road ahead, such as obstacles and potholes, there is a danger that a rider will fall and take down those around them. It is at this point that trust becomes more important than competence. If a bond of trust holds the group together, then competence can be built on it. A culture of supporting and caring for one another is more important than technical competence or, in our case, riding ability.

Each of our riders, regardless of their riding skill, experience or ability, is elevated by the trust that is quickly built within the group. Their confidence and competence grows exponentially, knowing they can trust those they are riding alongside.

It is at this point that trust becomes more important than competence. If a bond of trust holds the group together, then competence can be built on it.

The basis for building trust on our rides is consistency. Having ridden with hundreds of different riders over the years, I very quickly form an opinion on who I trust to ride behind and who I will peel away from when they take the lead. It has nothing to do with competence and everything to do with consistency. If I'm riding behind an experienced rider and they fail to call out obstacles on the road, their technical ability, strength and experience become irrelevant. It is their lack of consistency that puts me at risk.

Building trust within our tribes, whether at work with colleagues or clients or in our personal relationships, relies on our consistently showing up for others. In chapter 4 I talk about the importance of presence and the need to be there for your team. I present a case that as a leader you don't have to have all the answers, you don't even have to bring about change, but you do need to demonstrate that you care and understand the challenges. Nothing in that is inconsistent with the lessons on the road. Be present, be consistent, be reliable, and you will build strong teams and a culture that survives the greatest challenges.

There is a practice on our rides that when the strongest and fastest riders arrive at the end of each stage, they turn around and ride back to the last rider and simply accompany them for the remaining kilometres to the water stop. That signals to the riders at the back of the pack that the end of the stage is close and it raises their energy levels again. This builds morale and an esprit de corps that binds together the members of the group, inspiring enthusiasm, solidarity and a shared regard for the honour of the group.

Be present, be consistent, be reliable, and you will build strong teams and a culture that survives the greatest challenges.

During 2005 when I was not in Thailand on deployment with the identification work, I contributed to the selection of the teams that would travel to Thailand. The ones I sought out as a priority were those who consistently showed up for the team they worked with. I wasn't looking for the most experienced or the most technically gifted. A base level of technical competence and forensic expertise was a given, but the best teams were made up of those who were there for one another, those who consistently showed up. Working in those physically and mentally challenging environments, consistency and culture trumped competence.

On my first ride back in July 2022, some two and a half years after the last ride pre-COVID, I personally felt deep gratitude that I was back riding along the coastal foreshore of Thailand, with the warmth of the sun on my arms, the sounds of the roosters in the fields, the distant buzz of motorbikes, which when they approached didn't roar past us at frightening speed but crept past with the rider dipping their head in a customary acknowledgement, almost an apology.

> *Working in those physically and mentally challenging environments, consistency and culture trumped competence.*

If gratitude was a strong feeling in the group, presence was too. There seemed to be an unspoken desire in the group — and certainly I felt it — to be present in what we were doing, where we were and who we were with. At times I am so guilty of physically being in these wonderful places, but mentally being somewhere else, thinking of 'what's next'. This time felt different. I felt truly present, connected to the place and those I was riding with. I hope that with the passage of time these feelings don't pass too quickly. I hope I remain present and grateful for the joyful life I lead.

WHAT I HAVE LEARNED

Adversity, challenge and struggle have a way of uniting communities, bringing together those who might not otherwise meet, and creating bonds that can be understood only by those who are part of the experience.

Growth happens at the very edge of our limitations when we want to give up, feeling like we have no more to give, yet we choose to keep going anyway. Self-imposed limitations are not objective breaking points; they're just limits we set ourselves. Sharing a common goal or challenge with others elevates our own abilities and beliefs. We find we can achieve more than we imagine we are capable of.

WHAT CAN YOU DO?

Don't sit on the sidelines waiting until you have acquired the skill, experience or strength to 'keep up'. Just consistently show up. If you surround yourself with those who share your culture and bring the same level of integrity each day, you will soon fill any gaps in competency that may exist.

So you think about the thing you most want to do, achieve, experience or be, but self-doubt holds you back, knowing there are others who will do it better or faster than you. How about just showing up to start with? Then return and show up consistently and see what happens. Most often, the message you convey through consistently showing up will trump competence.

CHAPTER 12
PLAN YOUR EXIT STRATEGY FROM DAY ONE

At what point in our journey do we plan for our exit, whether from work, from the business we have created, the charity we launched, the movement we built over the years or the inescapable exit from life we all face? What does our 'redundancy' look like and how much energy do we commit to planning for it?

Starting a charity, building the foundations leading to the provision of services and to growth, is an interesting case, because the ultimate goal of all charities should be to cease to exist. Consider your favourite charity or a cause that is close to your heart and receives your financial and emotional support. Whether its focus is on caring for the homeless, feeding the hungry, supporting cancer survivors or, as in my case, supporting kids without parents who can care for them in either the short- or the long-term, the ultimate success would be for the problem itself to no longer exist.

For a charity that supports women surviving breast cancer, is the measure of their ultimate success that they are able to support twice the number of survivors they did the previous year or that they supported only half the number because advances in research were leading to earlier diagnosis and preventative care? Perhaps the remit of the charity is focused solely on supporting the survivors rather than on cancer research, but wouldn't they cheer any reduction in the need for their services and celebrate the day they closed their doors for lack of need?

Australia began mass vaccination against polio in 1956, and the country's last polio epidemic was in 1961–62. Australia was officially declared polio free in 2000. During the fight against polio many organisations were devoted to the prevention of the spread of the virus and support for those infected. As generations who live free of the virus we don't mourn the demise of these charities but celebrate the eradication of the disease. We applaud the work that has led to this eradication in all but two countries, Afghanistan and Pakistan.

Investing your heart and soul in a cause that you hope will one day cease to exist is an interesting if not unique exercise, but perhaps it gives us an insight when considering our own exit plans.

So long as the need exists, I would be deeply saddened to think that the services we have provided to the children and communities we support in Thailand ceased to exist. It would be nice to think that the problems that lead young mothers to abandon their children at bus stops, hospitals or temples could be addressed to prevent that occurring. It would be equally desirable that domestic violence behind closed doors that takes the lives of mothers and sends fathers to jail isn't an enduring problem, but it is. And while those and a myriad other causes exist there will be a need for charities like ours to support those left behind.

At *Hands* we work equally hard to support the children living in our care in celebrating the life of choice we create for them as to support those whose changed circumstances allow the reunification of previously broken families. Even when, on first view, it appears that the children living in our homes have a brighter future based on education and opportunity, we hold firm to the belief that the best place for children when all else is equal is with their family. We know that a degree, a trade or a career doesn't trump the love and learning a family can offer.

One measure of the success of a leader is knowing when to step aside and ensuring a smooth transition.

So how do you invest your heart and soul into something that one day by design will not exist, and if you do your job properly the end will be by your own doing? Personally, I can't foresee a time during my life when *Hands* no longer has a positive role to play in Thailand. The direction and focus may change, as it has done over the past 20 years, but I firmly believe in the long-term positive contribution we continue to make. The decision for me personally, then, is not about ending the charity I started, but about ending my role in it.

A good leader invests time and energy in fostering a successor. One measure of the success of a leader is knowing when to step aside and ensuring a smooth transition. What stops a leader from stepping down and handing over control?

Founder's syndrome kicks in when the founder of an organisation has difficulty in relinquishing control. They tend to believe that the organisation won't or can't exist without them and are dismissive of others' ideas. In this way the inspiration, influence and personality of the founder that was responsible for giving birth to the organisation becomes detrimental to its evolution and growth.

Judging when a leader should remove themselves partially or totally for the future benefit of the organisation is tricky, and finding that balance involves a lot of soul searching and an acceptance that others can and might well do a better job. The risk of introducing significant change in the modus operandi too quickly is that an organisation can lose its DNA, the building blocks of its tribe, the culture and the movement, the very core of what made it successful in the first place, but without the courage to let go, to change, its true potential may never be realised.

In the not-for-profit space the challenge for many small to medium-sized organisations is in finding a leader who not only has the capabilities of the founder, but who is willing to invest the same amount of time and energy for what is often well below the level of financial remuneration they could attract elsewhere. You don't start a charity to get rich, that's for sure, and the ledger is most often well in favour of the organisation in terms of your personal investment of time and effort. If you don't start a charity to get rich, you don't join a charity to increase your earnings either.

Dan Pallotta, in the TED talk I have referred to a number of times in this book, talks about how relatively poorly remunerated leaders in the not-for-profit space are and how this inhibits the attraction of the best talent. When it comes time to replace the founder, much thought should be given to the 'cost' of their inspiration, influence and commitment, not because of the position they held, but with a thought for the belief and passion with which they built the organisation in the first place. Does that mean we can't be replaced or we're always the best person to lead the organisation forward? Of course not.

My personal challenge in *Hands* is finding the balance between knowing when is the right time to step down from the role I currently occupy and creating the space for my successor to step in and set their own direction. My own self-awareness tells me a successful transition would mean my stepping back and allowing the future leader complete and autonomous control, with the oversight of a board.

The prospect of having little or no involvement in the direction and work of *Hands* is both exciting and scary. Without question I derive enormous personal benefit from my involvement with *Hands*. I have said many times that my life has been richer on every level since my decision to start the organisation. But the sense of responsibility I feel for the generation of income to meet our responsibilities in Thailand is heavy, and never more so than in recent years.

There is a talented and devoted team working for *Hands* who are committed to our goals, but when a ride doesn't recruit the numbers we hoped or a campaign falls short of our projections, I feel responsible. The success of what we have created has only added to my sense of responsibility. It is not mine alone to shoulder, but ultimately I feel accountable to those who donate and those who rely on our support.

Our success means the recurrent funding we need has risen from an initial $50 000 to over $2 million per annum. The more we raise, the more support we can deliver, which creates ever greater dependency, which means we need to raise still more. There are certainly days when I would happily hand over that responsibility, but how would I feel if I stepped aside and the new leadership decided to drop the bike rides or close the university scholarship program or exit Thailand completely?

Would changes in direction by a new leader represent the pursuit of untapped opportunities or refined and better operating systems, or would they be about putting their own stamp on the organisation and therefore represent something more personal?

The more we raise, the more support we can deliver, which creates ever greater dependency, which means we need to raise still more.

During the tours of Thailand following the tsunami the executive leadership team charged with leading the international identification process was working on four- to six-week rotations. By April 2005 the Joint Chiefs of Staff who reported to the Thai Police Commander implemented a decision that the most senior positions of responsibility in Thailand could only be filled by returning leaders.

No new leaders could occupy the most senior positions in Thailand unless that had previously performed at least one rotation in an international leadership role. The rationale for the decision was that with each new change in command the leader was introducing change to the process or system they had inherited, as leaders do. However, with a turnover in leadership every four weeks the constant change was impeding progress, not contributing to it. By restricting the leadership roles to those of us who had previously completed tours of duty there was a level of continuity in leaders that brought consistency and predictability, which is always desirable when working in challenging environments.

The path to success is developing a clear and agreed exit plan and abiding by it. And it needs to be based on respect—for the history and accumulated knowledge, but equally for the authority of the new leadership team to make different decisions and take the business in a different direction.

How does the new leader grapple with the challenge of leading an organisation when the previous leader has been especially charismatic and influential? This was certainly the challenge faced by the new director at Baan Tharn Namchai to replace Khun Rotjana. Across my two careers I'm not sure I have met anyone who was as charismatic as Khun Rotjana. She had the ability to mix it with all levels of society and make them feel comfortable in her presence. But of course her favourite place was with the kids at BTN.

As Khun Rotjana became increasingly unwell during 2017 it was clear to her, her team and those of us who had worked with her over the previous decade that whoever took over the role of director at BTN had a daunting task. In the months and weeks before her death she indicated to me that her pick was not from among her current staff but rather one of her former students, Game.

Game had come to BTN in the very early years to escape a house filled with alcohol and violence. He had been given an ultimatum that if he wanted to remain living in the house he was in he would need to leave school and get a job to pay his own way. If he wanted to remain at school or couldn't find a job to cover his costs, he would have to move out. He was 12 years old. In informing the school that he would have to leave and find a job, a teacher who saw the potential in Game asked Khun Rotjana if she had room for one more student. Of course she said yes.

Game joined the other students at BTN and promised to repay Khun Rotjana in any way he could. She effectively became the mother he had never had. When Khun Rotjana called on Game to return to the home as its director, he of course agreed. Truth be told, I think he would have done anything that Khun Rotjana asked of him to repay her and honour her legacy.

Returning to BTN as director and in charge of the staff who had once been his teachers was a challenge and a burden he struggled with. To be honest, he didn't seek the role, didn't aspire to it and didn't want it, but he did it to honour the legacy and dying wishes of a woman he loved more than anyone. He loved the kids, but the job involved so much more than spending time with them.

I'm not sure Khun Rotjana appreciated the depth of the challenge and struggle that lay ahead for Game, and I wonder, had she known what he would face in those first couple of years, if she would have asked so much of someone so young. Perhaps she believed the challenge and struggle would shape him into the person he would become. It was surely the case that the struggle he was facing was not because he was doing something wrong but because he was doing something right.

The leadership exhibited by Khun Game could not have stood in greater contrast to that of Khun Rotjana. The commonality between them was their undying love for the children they supported. The interesting thing that we observed over the first five years of his leadership was how he was slowly, almost by stealth, creating his own culture. There was no dramatic change. Perhaps that was out of respect for what Khun Rotjana had created, perhaps it was due to a lack of confidence. But slowly he evolved his own leadership style, one that saw greater transparency and accountability, one that relied less on charisma and more on process and collaboration, one that certainly appealed more to the board of *Hands*.

Khun Rotjana's charisma could never be matched, but the continuity of care for the kids serves to illustrate that everyone *has a limited tenure in the role they occupy.*

Before her untimely passing it would have been hard to imagine anyone other than Khun Rotjana leading BTN. If we had sought to make a succession plan we would have been justifiably concerned as to the future operations of the home. Now, more than five years on, the home continues to provide a loving and safe environment for the children, and if anything the reporting and management of the home have improved. Khun Rotjana's charisma could never be matched, but the continuity of care for the kids serves to illustrate that *everyone* has a limited tenure in the role they occupy.

If there is one organisation that is inseparable from its founder, it is Baan Home Hug. For as long as I have known her, the founder and director of that home, Mae Thiew, has faced personal health battles that often leave her weak and bedridden. Her greatest fear is not for herself but for the children and staff she will leave behind. She battles cancer in her own way and many times I have said goodbye at the end of a visit wondering if indeed I would see her alive again. But her will to live, and to live a life of service to the children in her care, seems inexhaustible. Still, her time will come, as it will for all of us.

No one worries more and prepares more for her passing than Mae Thiew. Her concern is not for her own death but for the impact of her absence. Her greatest, irreducible worry is that *Hands*, the biggest contributor to her home's recurrent operating costs, will leave when she is no longer there. For more than a decade now we have provided the financial support she needs to care for the children, to pay the staff, and to operate the home and meet the medical costs of many of the highly dependent children. Yet her worry is seemingly no less today than a decade ago.

The love and respect I have for Mae Thiew is beyond measure. I wonder what more I can do to give her peace of mind. It would be the greatest act of disloyalty to end our support for the children in the event of her death. She still worries about the future of the children and who will take over from her. Who will assume that responsibility? I see the staff at BHH and I understand her concern, but when we look at BTN and how it has grown under Khun Game I am confident that while there is no obvious successor today, perhaps that is because no one could or would step up while she remains willing and able.

She is preparing for a future without her, though. I see it in her actions. She is building new, small homes for some of the boys who have autism on a level that makes living independently difficult. She is creating small-scale agricultural projects that give the boys skills and jobs now, but more importantly something to sustain them in the future. She is actively divesting herself of the responsibility of providing for the children, and in doing so is creating independence for them.

She is making it less about her and more about the ability of the home and the children to carry on without her. Each new market garden, coffee shop or fish farm she builds is to create skills in the children, to encourage new thinking and learning, and to look for that income stream that depends not on her and not on *Hands* or anyone else. As a true leader looking to create the greatest legacy she can, she is seeking to make herself irrelevant and replaceable. Perhaps the greatest gift she can give the children is their independence, and before her time runs out she knows that if the kids and the home can live without her or *Hands* or any independent funder, then her work is done. If the children are the custodians of their own future, if there are enough sustainable projects in place to meet the needs of those incapable of providing for themselves, then that security and certainly can't be taken away, withheld or withdrawn.

As a true leader looking to create the greatest legacy she can, she is seeking to make herself irrelevant and replaceable.

I often think about the exit plans of Khun Rotjana and Mae Thiew, and how they have, in their different ways, approached their imminent and potential absence. Of course, Khun Rotjana was given a much shorter time to prepare, as her deterioration in mind and body was swift. Khun Rotjana chose Game to take over her leadership. Mae Thiew has sought to create structures that do not need a charismatic leader and that bring the control and power back to those in her care. In effect, the older kids become responsible for their own destiny and future, without the need to rely on others to provide for them and meet their needs.

In building organisations, movements, charities or followings, how much of the role of the leader is about our personal ego? Our ego wants us to be missed and for chaos to reign in the event of our absence as a clear demonstration of just how important we were. My personal struggle with my future at *Hands* is based on a belief that I have a level of knowledge of *Hands* and its history that is unmatched. I believe I have a distribution channel and personal commitment to the cause that will be hard to equal, but how much of that is really about me and the notion that I am more special than I actually am? Wouldn't the greatest thing I could do as a leader for the future of *Hands* be not to seek out someone to replace me but to make my role redundant? To create new channels of distribution to focus not on the history but on the future.

Mae Thiew is creating a future that is not dependent on her or what she does. Ultimately she will be missed not for what she did but for who she was. There will be grief, overwhelming sadness and a deep sense of loss, but if she continues on her current path there will be relatively little impact on operations and there will be certainty for the children. Is that not the ultimate role of the leader, a perfect demonstration of selfless leadership?

> *Ultimately she will be missed not for what she did but for who she was.*

Of course, there are organisations in which it is not only improbable but impractical for a leader to divest themselves of responsibility. What, then, for those leaders and their exit strategy, and when should that planning start? Perhaps the appropriate day to start planning your exit is your first day in the role. If each leader sees it is a fundamental part of their job to actively develop their successor, to impart knowledge, to provide counsel, to mentor and build a competent replacement, they are building trust from day one with those who might aspire to their job.

There is nothing admirable in a leader who holds back knowledge in order to maintain a power advantage over those they lead. Rather, I think it is a clear sign of weakness and vulnerability, an admission of their insecurity. Such leaders clearly believe that knowledge is power, and that is all they have to cling on to.

Nothing in a leader better conveys personal confidence than their willingness to share all they know with those who aspire to their job and will in all likelihood succeed them. There is no better way for a leader to build loyalty within their team than by devoting themselves to enriching their team members' lives and creating pathways to their success.

WHAT I HAVE LEARNED

We like to feel wanted and needed, to feel we make a difference. We feed our ego with the self-centred thought that what we do is unique. We tell ourselves that no one else could possibly do what we do. Or if there is someone, they are so special that we are going to have to pay them a truckload of cash, because that represents *our* true worth.

I reflect on what Mae Thiew is doing with each new little project she opens that can be managed by the kids. When she gives one of the autistic boys four buffalo to look after, she is creating a sense of responsibility in him. For as long as he has his buffalo he has meaning, purpose and a job. He can create income, and he needs Mae Thiew a little less each day. When we work unselfishly towards making ourselves redundant, we become more relevant as a leader than ever before. Our legacy is less about what we did and the hole created by our absence and more about who we were and the strength and stability we created before we left.

WHAT CAN YOU DO?

In actively working to build up others to succeed us, we become the leader who is needed and valued most by the organisation. We build succession, focusing on continuity in order to avoid disruption in our absence. We're also valued by our team as we work with integrity to create opportunities for them at our own expense. Where do the opportunities exist in your life to build others up and reduce their reliance and dependence on you? How can you build towards your own redundancy by empowering those around you?

CHAPTER 13
ADOPT A LIMITLESS MINDSET

If asked to share our dreams with a room full of people we don't know, most of us are likely to balk. A big part of that is the fear that people will judge us. At what point do we decide what we are capable of rather than allowing others to impose their limiting beliefs on us?

When we look at those we admire based on their achievements, we're usually drawn to them only after their achievements have been recognised. Think of someone you would love to hang out with, have as a 'favourite' on your phone or just admire from a distance. Is it a sportsperson, a musician, a global CEO, a filthy-rich entrepreneur or someone you know who has achieved something pretty remarkable?

You have no doubt been drawn to them out of admiration for the achievements they have stacked up. You admire these achievements and perhaps even have a mild desire to do something similar. More likely, you tell yourself that, for a long list of reasons, you could never do what they have done. When we hold those beliefs, allowing that internal dialogue to persist, we talk down our abilities, limit what's possible for us and forgo the chance to do or be what we really want. Is it the fear of failure in the eyes of others or our own harsh judgement of ourselves that gets in the way? Or both?

At what point do we decide what we are capable of rather than allowing others to impose their limiting beliefs on us?

For me, 2019 was a year in which I determined to take on a couple of new challenges. Neither played any part in my professional development, and neither would lead me towards a new career. I certainly didn't need to do either. But the way I managed them speaks to my fear of being judged should I not succeed. My first challenge was to learn to fly a helicopter. Not a plane. I hate flying in small planes. I don't fear them, I just don't enjoy them. The bigger the better for me.

During my time in the police I had flown a lot in the back seat of the police helicopter PolAir on various jobs, especially when I was stationed in Tamworth. We could request their services for various jobs, and as I worked only in major crime our requests were never knocked back. It was just a matter of scheduling. I always enjoyed the physical sensation of the take-off and how manoeuvrable they were. They just seemed like a whole lot of fun to fly. So with Claire's encouragement I started taking lessons. I was pretty shit, I reckon. Learning to hover, which engages a muscle memory you need to develop rather than something you learn, happens to be the trickiest part of learning to fly a heli. I would return from a lesson with the instructor sure that he would place a hand on my shoulder and suggest I find another hobby.

But I kept going, sat the written exams and got my licence in 2021. Here's the thing, though. I didn't tell a soul other than Claire that I was taking lessons, just in case that tap on the shoulder did come and I would become known as the person who took lessons but didn't crack it. What would be wrong with that? If I had tried and not succeeded, would anyone other than me really care? I think not. It's not like the kids at school were going to tease me! Learning to fly hasn't changed my life dramatically. It is something I absolutely love and flying friends and family to a vineyard for lunch or up the coast from Sydney is something I will never tire of. Flying over the southern pylon of the Sydney Harbour Bridge at 500 feet is incredible. It's a stunning harbour from any angle but better still from 500 feet.

If I had tried and not succeeded, would anyone other than me really care? I think not.

The second thing I did in 2019 was take up ultra-marathon running, which took me into the bush for the best part of a day and night. Again, not an essential activity and I'm never going to turn that into a career—I'm probably 30 years too late for that. Having spent plenty of time riding my bike over long distances, with several 200 km plus days, including a 270 km ride on my own in Thailand one day, I thought I would give the ultra a bit of a go. Speed was never going to be my thing, but I was drawn to the longer events and the ultra seemed like the next logical step.

One of the biggest learnings I have taken from ultra-marathons is the need to manage your energy, and by that I mean the mindset that you bring to and maintain during the run. The ultra might start or finish in the dark, or it might start *and* finish in the dark, depending on how long I am out there. But with such an endurance event you are pretty much guaranteed to move through a number of emotional spaces. When you toe the line at the start of the event you know you are in for a long day, no matter what happens, and when you are a plodder like me it can be a *very* long day.

There is incredible energy at the start of the run. Most runners will have spent a good six to nine months training and preparing, so the energy is palpable. You leave the start line in a swarm, and it's important not to get caught up in the emotion and take off too quickly. Within an hour or two, though, you will usually find you have the track pretty much to yourself. Runners will pass you and you will pass others — for me, it is more often the former than the latter, but generally you end up with clear air around you.

You will find yourself in a grind and as the kilometres tick by you know there is plenty of hard work to be done. The energy of the start will have dissipated and the best you can look forward to is being greeted by enthusiastic volunteers at the next fuel station. Normally, this is where I find my energy drops, and when the fuel station is a couple of hours away it can become really hard work. You may have a niggle, a blister, some hip pain, an upset tummy or all of the above. Your energy declines and then the voices in your head start telling you what a stupid idea this was.

But those times pass. The voice is filling your head with negative chat, but that too will pass. Sometimes it's just taking the next five minutes at a time or focusing on one kilometre at a time. When you are hurting and you focus on the 30 kilometres still to run, it can feel unachievable. But, barring a race-ending injury, we can all manage another five minutes of moving forward or another five hundred metres. Working through and embracing the discomfort, we find, for no particular reason, the negative chat has ended and the dark mood has gone with it.

The voice is filling your head with negative chat, but that too will pass.

Kirrily Dear, an outstanding Australian, has completed some absolutely epic runs. She has a saying: 'Fitness doesn't determine if you reach the finish line, it only reduces the suffering.' She would know, having completed, among a stack of other challenges, a solo run from Broken Hill to Sydney, which is a lazy 1000 km run or thereabouts. So if it's not fitness that gets you to the finish line, and we are guessing that plays some part in a 1000 km run, what is it?

I asked Kirrily that question. If it wasn't all about fitness, what was it about? Her response offered a priceless insight. She said, 'The short answer is the frame of mind with which you approach the task, but what specifically about mindset will determine success? If I had to narrow it down to one thing it would be your relationship with the fear and self-doubt that will emerge during the journey. All actions that you take start in your mind—you think, then do—and it's through that process that your mind regulates the performance of your body. If your mind doesn't believe you can do the task, then it will shut down your activity, to conserve and protect your body.'

Consider what Kirrily has done—look it up, it's massive—and what Ned Brockmann did in 2022, running across Australia. These ultra-athletes complete these incredible feats not because they have trained to avoid the pain, not even because they are adopting a mindset that is limitless, but because they have found a way to embrace the discomfort and pain that is a part of such events. Certainly their mindset around limitations, whether imposed by self or by others, is very different from what most of us accept. Exceptional people simply reject the limitations that most of us believe are fixed boundaries and choose to go further.

If you sign up for some wild adventure that will test your perceived physical limits, and you do so without expecting to visit the hurt locker, then when it comes time to step into it you're unprepared and ill-equipped to deal with it. Those who are prepared know the pain will come and when it arrives they welcome it, like an annoying uncle who comes to stay, makes life unpleasant for a while but then leaves. You just suck it up and laugh at all those jokes you've heard before.

··

Exceptional people simply reject the limitations that most of us believe are fixed boundaries and choose to go further.

··

A real learning for me as I do more and more ultras is not to be surprised when it gets shitty. I know that each time I cross the start line there will be difficult times on the track and if I am ready for them mentally, if I accept that they are going to come, then I can just continue to move forward. Crossing the line on completing my first ultra, past the amazing crowd who line the finishers tunnel, was an experience I'll never forget. I was tapped out, with little left in the tank, and I had been through some shitty times on the trail, but here was the finish. I had made it.

The euphoric feeling of crossing the line remains one I look forward to. I turned up for an ultra not long after they resumed following the COVID shutdowns. I had been in peak condition four months out and ready to tackle 100 km through the glorious Blue Mountains. Within that four months I had picked up COVID, got sick and lost the will and desire to train. Turning up for the run after a delayed start I was well underdone. I knew it was going to hurt more than the others. I also knew I had the choice of withdrawing at any time before or during the race should I wish to. No one but me would care or even notice.

I completed the run. Lots of it wasn't all that enjoyable but crossing the line it made up for the pain I felt on the trail and as soon as I finished the pain was gone, until I had to walk two additional kilometres to the car.

The trick to embracing our wildest dreams or goals is we just need to start. There is a risk that we look at the end as something that is unattainable and therefore keep putting off starting or, worse still, never do. We can find plenty of excuses to put things off because the time is not right. But every time we say no to something that is important to us, a little part of us dies. We need to focus on the results and not the excuses.

One compelling reason a lot of busy parents forgo or put off tackling these adventures for themselves is time. With all the demands of parenting active kids, there's just not time for much else. What with all the out-of-school activities, plenty of parents are doing their best just to keep afloat. A day in the life of a busy mum can be like running a marathon each day.

The trick to embracing our wildest dreams or goals is we just need to start.

I don't pretend to know what it is like to have school-age kids anymore—mine are well beyond that—and I wouldn't presume to preach to parents about what they should do. I have seen enough examples, though, of how the relationship between parent and child or the entire family can benefit when time is committed to the pursuit of something amazing that is hugely important to all involved.

Consider the example you are setting for your kids when they see you committing time to pursuing your own dreams. I have talked about the mums who have joined our rides and how in the preparation they have found a new, invaluable shared experience for the family as they ride and train together.

More than a couple of times on rides mums have told me that the response of their kids to mum riding with us in Thailand is one of pride. They are proud of your journey—the training, the commitment, the fundraising and seeing it all through. Being told by your children that they are proud of you is a powerful thing. Beyond endorsement and encouragement, it is different from expressions of love and probably not something we say often other than to kids under the age of 10. And here's the thing. When mums share that story with me, guess the emotion that is gushing through their body? It's pride and self-acknowledgement.

Being told by your children that they are proud of you is a powerful thing.

Hands is now approaching its twentieth anniversary, and we have chalked up a few not insignificant achievements. If you measure us in terms of dollars raised, it would be fair to say that exceeding $30 million in that time is a notable achievement. Supporting more than 30 kids through graduation at university is another. And we can point to the immeasurable difference we have made at Baan Home Hug with the HIV kids—yes, there are some big ticks right there.

I have talked with many people during Q&A sessions or after I have presented at conferences and have received much kind acknowledgement of what we have achieved at *Hands*. But of course it all started with that phone conversation with Gill in the kitchen. If she had asked, 'Are you willing to commit the next 20 years of your life to the kids in Thailand, to stop these kids dying of HIV at Baan Home Hug, to lead more than thirty 500 km or 800 km fundraising bike rides and raise over $30 million for the cause? Are you up for that?', I wouldn't have thought it was a serious conversation. I never would have signed up for that because I never would have believed I could have achieved any of those things.

'Don't ride the hills before you get there.'

The reason I would have thought it was crazy was I was focusing on the end, or where we are now, rather than what we needed to do in the first month, then six months then twelve months. Focusing on the start was doable. Then you blink and the next thing you know 20 years have passed and the amazing community of *Hands Across the Water* has flowered. Not an aspirational statement, a fact.

We have a saying on our rides: 'Don't ride the hills before you get there.' I think it is a message for life. If we worry about the hills ahead, there's a good chance we won't ride at all or we'll be so anxious that we won't enjoy the experience. It is one of the few frustrating things that occur on our rides in Thailand. When those who have done the ride before talk about the hills, it can spook the new riders so they spend so much time worrying about what is to come that they fail to enjoy the here and now. The hills don't get easier because you worry about them, but they sure can impact your experience before you get there.

On our Coastal Ride we leave from Bangkok and ride south down through a number of towns on the Gulf of Thailand, before crossing over to the west coast and the Andaman Sea. On the morning of day eight, our final day on the bike, just 11 km out from of the hotel, there is a hill that is 4.2 km long. If you ride like you're being chased by a grizzly bear you can get to the top in just over 10 minutes. If you take your time checking out the scenery, stopping for a photo or two, we'll see you at the top in about 25 minutes. But here's the thing. Riders who are new to the Coastal Ride will spend days and nights worrying about this hill, which at best lasts 10 minutes and at worst 25 minutes. I have people decide which ride they will do based on this particular hill.

Fun fact: Everyone makes it to the top of this hill, and they do so because they start. They climb onto their bike, clip into the pedals, select a low gear and point their front wheel in the direction of the top of the hill. And they get there — always.

Once at the top of the hill they often comment that it wasn't nearly as bad as they thought it would be. Things seldom are. Yet we so often overthink them, talk ourselves down, undervalue our abilities and allow others to impose their limiting thoughts. How often are the negative judgements of others about our dreams and goals more a reflection of their limited beliefs than our ability? One hundred per cent of the time, I reckon.

I have always loved this quote from T.E. Lawrence: 'All men dream; but not equally. Those who dream by night in the dusty recesses of their minds awake to find that it was vanity. But the dreamers of day are dangerous men. That they may act their dreams with open eyes to make it possible.'

We need dreamers and we all need to dream a little more. As Sarah Ban Breathnach, author of *Simple Abundance*, says, 'The world needs dreamers and the world needs doers. But above all, the world needs dreamers who do.'

So what stops us from taking action or, more important, what would we benefit from doing to give ourselves a greater shot at having a go? Because success shouldn't be measured simply by the attainment of a dream or goal, but by the fact that we gave it a red-hot crack in the first place. Then, when we put our head on the pillow at night, at least we know we pointed that front wheel towards the hill and gave it our best.

I've often reflected on the journeys of successful people as well as considering my own path with the building of *Hands*, and I've found that there are similarities in approach between building the largest contributing Australian charity to Thailand and getting myself ready for an ultra through the bush. The following points may serve you well when considering committing to your own audacious goal or dream. Sometimes what's needed is just a paradigm shift in our thinking. As Kirrily has pointed out, the body will often follow what the mind believes.

1. Understand what you need to do, create or plan to get started. The end goal may be on the vision board, and you need to connect with this as the thing that gets you out of bed early in the morning to train when the weather is indifferent. But you need to make the starting easy.

2. Measure what you do so you can monitor change and progress. Set milestones that allow you to celebrate success or simply the fact that you are still in the fight.

3. No one is going to believe in you as much as you need them to. Get ready for the doubters, the knockers, and

those who don't want you to succeed and may try to
sabotage you. You need to be your strongest believer. If
you leave that job to someone else and they leave, that can
compromise your entire dream. Own it.

4. Construct shared agendas to solve complex problems.
   Getting a team on board who offer wisdom, counsel,
   backing and experience can accelerate your growth
   and help you avoid the mistakes that are normally only
   revealed in the doing. But ensure you find the balance
   between listening and acting on their advice to avoid
   having the mission drift away from your dream.

5. Be the courageous leader we have spoken about. You will
   need to make some tough decisions and take risks that
   may put it all on the line. But with risk comes reward.
   Remember, our greatest innovators and artists operate
   outside the parameters of what's accepted and safe.

6. Know that it can take time, and the hardest part will be
   operating without credibility. It is easier to sell your dream
   to backers, investors or donors when you can say, 'This is
   what we have previously done with the funds', rather than,
   'This is what I hope to do'. You must take a lot of risk;
   your sponsors or donors, not so much. You will need to be
   patient and be prepared to tell your story a lot!

7. Regularly take time to analyse where you are and where
   you are going. Now you've launched and are in it up
   to your eyeballs, has your dream or vision changed?
   Remember that the wrong decision is better than no
   decision; it is perfectly fine to adjust and keep adjusting
   until you get to where you need to be.

8. Sometimes our greatest victories are achieved when we
   believe we are right at the edge of what is possible. When

you think you have no more to give, you're probably only about half way done. Find five more minutes, and turn up again tomorrow.

9. Once you've got there, look at how you can improve, or do more. The thrill is in the pursuit and if you don't keep growing you lose your edge and stagnate.

Nelson Mandela said, 'There is no passion to be found playing small and settling for a life that is less than the one you're capable of living.' No one else is going to make this happen for you, or if they are, is it really *your* wildest dream you're pursuing or are you just jumping on board someone else's dream? If no one else is creating the space for this dream to occur, regardless of what it is, then be the one to take control and live your life accordingly.

WHAT I HAVE LEARNED

Success cannot be judged by the validation of followers we have never met. Living life well is the feeling we get when we are in pursuit of our wildest dreams. We know we're there when we can't describe how good it is. When those sitting life out don't understand what we're on about, then we know we're probably in the right place, where we are meant to be.

Don't look to others for validation or endorsement, because there will always be plenty of people who will tell you why you can't do it, why it's beyond you, why you're too old, too young, too big or too small. F**k the lot of them, I say. It's your dream to pursue, and the best way to do that is to just start. Just take action that commits you to doing something scary and audacious.

Creating time in your busy life for yourself, at the expense of time shared with others, is not selfish. When you live a conventional life that rules out the pursuit of dreams, you are denying the best of you to those you love the most. We think we don't have enough time, and in part we're right. Life passes so quickly that we absolutely don't have enough time to give up on our dreams and goals. We imagine we'll pursue these challenges later on, when we're freer. But when does that time come? Having seen more than my share of death in my life, if I have learned anything it is that we only get one go at life and we owe it to ourselves to seize it.

WHAT CAN YOU DO?

Just start ...

CONCLUSION

We won't always succeed or even finish the things we start. But we have zero chance of either winning or finishing if we don't start. Self-doubt, limiting beliefs and the negative chat of others are serious inhibitors of success, as too is waiting until we have the answers to all the possible questions before we start.

Writing this book has given me cause to pause and reflect on the *Leaders, Achievers and Visionaries* who have so positively impacted my life. If they have one common denominator, it is that they are just normal people who committed to a task that often started out small and, with the continued application of their tenacious will and wisdom, turned into something remarkable. Reflecting on the attributes of those I have written about, it is not their technical skill or wisdom that stands out; it is their compassion, their commitment and their resolve.

Legacies are created and books are written about those who find a reason to say yes rather than put forward excuses. We don't remember the names of those who had a good idea but it remained that, an idea. We admire those who commit to a cause without certainty of success, and even more those for whom success was less likely or more improbable, but who achieved it in spite of the obstacles.

Don't wait for your self-belief to manifest or for the certainty that you will prevail. Great leaders continue to reach for more, do more and create more, never feeling satisfied that they have 'arrived'. A belief that what you are doing is the right thing to do at the right time is sufficient for you to make decisions with integrity and good intent.

Leaders, Achievers and Visionaries are of course rarely independent of one another. Remember Sarah Ban Breathnach: 'The world needs dreamers and the world needs doers. But above all, the world needs dreamers who do.' Many of those I write about here play a role in all three parts of the book. Perhaps our greatest leaders are visionaries and the great achievers are indeed the leaders of our time.

Our visions and dreams are ours alone, until they are shared. We can seldom realise them alone, but sharing them makes them real. No matter how audacious their dream or vision, great leaders and great achievers find a way to share it and inspire others. Whether driving forward a company or a country, all great leaders share certain qualities:

- They genuinely care about the people they lead.
- They have a shared and known purpose.
- They are present.
- They accept and manage risk, while challenging process and boundaries.
- They embrace innovation and creativity.
- They find opportunities to say yes more often than no.

Don't wait for the 'right' time to do the things you long to do, because that time may never come. If not now, when? If not you, who?

I wish you well in your journey as a Leader, Achiever and Visionary.

Pete

THAI NAMES AND PLACES

Baan Home Hug. The home we started supporting in 2010 located in the Isan region of northeast Thailand. It was home to over one hundred children, many dealing with significant health issues when we first took them in.

Baan Nam Khem. The location of the tsunami refuge centre we built in 2010. It also serves as a community centre and up until February 2023 it operated as a kindergarten for the local community. It now forms part of our Hospitality Training Centre and Bike Ride Centre. The area was badly hit by the tsunami as it is surrounded by water on three sides and the highest point is no more than a few metres above sea level. A wonderful museum and memorial to tsunami victims is now open to the public.

Baan Tharn Namchai. Shortened to BTN, this was the first home we built in the aftermath of the tsunami. It was originally built to house 32 kids, with the funding for the first, original building coming from a number of local and international sources.

Khru. The courtesy title for *teacher* in Thai.

Khru Prateep. The creator of the Duang Prateep Foundation who opened her foundation in 1978 to support the communities and children of the slums of Thailand.

Khun. The courtesy title used to show respect in Thai. It precedes the first name and is used for both men and women.

Khun Rotjana. The first Director of Baan Tharn Namchai, who had travelled from Bangkok for a planned two years to support the children left without parents. She never left. We lost Khun Rotjana to cancer on December 24, 2017.

Klong Toei. A slum community in central Bangkok where more than 100 000 people live. When Bangkok's port was built many labourers from villages outside the city were enticed into the city for work, attracted by wages beyond anything they could make on the farms. After the work at the port authority ended, many remained in the area that had become their home. Generations of these people have called the slum of Khlong Toei home. Over the past 10 years I have led many corporate programs into the slums, where we knocked down homes and employed the locals to build new ones. This brought employment to those with the desire to make their community better. For as long as I have been visiting the country, the Thai Government has had on the table a proposal of one type or another to reclaim what is now valuable land and evict those who live there. To date, no government has been effective in bringing change.

Mae. The courtesy title used for *mother* in Thai.

Mae Thiew. The Director of Baan Home Hug whom I first met in 2010 and who remains the source of inspiration to those who have met her.

Pama House. In 2015 we took responsibility for a home in the Chanthaburi province located in the east of Thailand. It is a small home that serves the community and was the destination for the 2023 January Ride to Provide, our first full ride after the COVID lay-off.

Tha Chat Chai. Located on Phuket Island on the southern side of the Sarasin Bridge linking the island to the mainland. This was the location of the disaster victim identification centre that was built in response to the tsunami and commenced operations in April 2005.

Wat Yan Yao. A temple located in the northern end of the town of Takua Pa in Phang Nga province. The resort area of Khao Lak is to the south of this area, and two hours' drive further south is the island of Phuket. The temple was the first place the deceased victims of the tsunami in Thailand were taken. It was here that the temporary mortuary was constructed and where many foreign and local visitors would descend in search of their loved ones.

ABOUT HANDS

Hands Across the Water is an international charity started after the devastating effects of the Boxing Day tsunami of 2004 left hundreds of children without families to care for them. The charity's original intent was to build a home for these children of Thailand, but upon opening the first home at Baan Tharn Namchai in the Khao Lak region of Thailand, it became clear that far more support was needed and this was merely the start of the journey.

In the first five years, the charity saw rapid growth, building various homes and centres to provide housing and shared facilities across the communities. By 2011, it had expanded to directly fund several centres across Thailand, including a home for children infected with HIV. In particular, this support helped to bring an end to the HIV-related deaths that had affected the centre for over two decades, prior to the charity's involvement.

From very early on, *Hands Across the Water*, today known simply as *Hands*, sought to engage with its donors and supporters on a deeper level than just seeking donations. Through its regular fundraising bike rides, the charity aims to create a value exchange where donors feel more connected to the cause, rather than just a relationship built on philanthropy and generosity. This approach allows *Hands* to offer a high level of transparency by showing donors how funds are raised and used, and also how this benefits the operation of the homes the charity supports.

At a governance level, the charity is aligned to, and works towards, the UN Sustainable Development Goals of 2030 and is compliant with, or is working towards, no fewer than eleven of those seventeen goals. *Hands* is very proud of its history of governance and compliance and this work has been recognised with the charity achieving tax deductibility status by the Governments of Australia, New Zealand and Thailand. This is a reflection of the charity's integrity and transparency since inception, and an endorsement by those government agencies of the work undertaken and method by which the funds have been raised and spent.

In support of the fundraising efforts, and to reduce the spend of donor's funds on administrative or fundraising costs, the charity operates two social enterprise companies in Australia and Thailand, respectively. These companies generate income through various commercial means and that income is then used to meet the operating costs of the charity.

The future of *Hands* is to keep one eye on the immediate needs of the children and another on the future. In the immediate, the charity's focus is to attend to the most basic needs of food, shelter, health care and education, and to ensure the homes they build or support are filled with love and respect, creating rich learning environments for the children in a safe place. In addition to meeting the immediate needs of the children and communities that *Hands* supports, the charity will look to build capacity on the ground in Thailand to generate income and ensure certainty of funding for the operating costs of the homes.

Hands' measure of success goes beyond the number of buildings built, funds raised or children supported. Ultimately, success for *Hands* is securing a child's future when they ultimately decide to leave the home. *Hands'* success is, instead, based on ensuring that the children in its care are able to live a life of choice, not chance. To achieve this success, the charity has invested heavily in a University Scholarship program that, at the time of printing, has enabled 33 children to graduate with degrees with a further 21 undertaking university study. *Hands* has also established a Digital Learning Centre and a Hospitality Training Centre, each of which will create increased employment opportunities not just for the children of *Hands* but for the broader community in which they operate.

To find out more, or to learn how you can help contribute to the future of *Hands,* visit handsacrossthewater.org.au.

Printed and bound by CPI Group (UK) Ltd, Croydon, CR0 4YY

04/08/2023

03243505-0001